T0275997

Sandy Britches and Sandy Toes:

My Jekyll Island Memories

By Jeff Foster

authorHOUSE®

AuthorHouse™
1663 Liberty Drive
Bloomington, IN 47403
www.authorhouse.com
Phone: 1 (800) 839-8640

Published by AuthorHouse 09/18/2019

ISBN: 978-1-7283-2804-1 (sc)
ISBN: 978-1-7283-2803-4 (e)

Library of Congress Control Number: 2019914494

To my beautiful wife Kathy, thank you for always
being by my side, no matter what.

I love you so very much.

CHAPTER ONE

How it all started

When I decided to write a book of my memories of Jekyll Island I wondered how I would start. Where would I begin? I sat in front of my computer screen and chewed on a pencil trying to figure it out. I remember my mother telling me many times the story of the first time she heard the name Jekyll Island and the first time she and my father went down to Jekyll. I decided, that would be a perfect beginning. My parents Jesse and Marie Foster never knew of Jekyll island or even where it was. When they first heard the name Jekyll Island my mother told me, all they could think was the 1941 movie thriller *Dr. Jekyll and Mr. Hyde* starring Spencer Tracy and Ingrid Bergman and the Magpie cartoon characters *Heckle and Jeckle*. As my mother told the story she said, "We didn't even know the island existed or where it was at until your father's brother Robert Foster, told us about it".

"Uncle Robert, Aunt Alice and their family always vacationed at Fort Clinch State Park in Fernandina Beach Florida. They took a day trip to Jekyll once after hearing about it themselves, enjoyed going and thought we might like it too. When they returned home Uncle Robert told us about their trip. The beaches were wide and uncrowded unlike parts of Florida and the wildlife was so tame that you could just about reach out and touch them! The motels were right on the beach. We decided then that it sounded like a place we'd like to go visit".

"The year was 1966 and we lived in Forest Park, Georgia about ten miles south of Atlanta. One day after your father returned home from work, we decided to take off and go visit this place called Jekyll Island. Stopping at the gas station your grandparents owned just down from our house we filled up the truck. We bought a map of the state of Georgia because we had no idea how to get there or how long it would take us to get there. Those were the days before Google maps and GPS.

"Late one afternoon, we set off in our old, black, Ford, pickup truck. Traveling down Interstate 75 we would usually get as far as Macon GA and end up getting lost and spend the night in a local motel. The next day we would get up, loose the desire to go any further, turn around and go back home to Forest Park. We went back and forth from home to Macon and back home a total of three times over a period of a few weeks. On the fourth time, we decided to go for it, kept going and finally made our way out of Macon. Following the map, we drove through South Georgia and went through many small towns." My mother also told me of the gas wars that the locally owned gas station owners in these small towns were waging against each other at the time. My mother told me later, "I am not sure why they even had these gas wars,. The gasoline was cheap enough back then."

Mom said," We made it to Brunswick in the middle of the night. Passing through downtown Brunswick, driving through the deserted streets, we saw signs pointing the way to Jekyll Island. We took many winding roads through the old neighborhoods lined with huge oak trees filled with Spanish moss hanging down like curtains covering the streetlights. We thought we were lost again until we made it to a roadway, which was highway 17. Turning right, we drove down this road over a huge draw bridge and finally saw a road sign that said Jekyll Island next left. Driving down the causeway past the entrance two towers, down a long two-lane road and over another smaller draw bridge; we finally made it onto the island."

"Once we got there, we had no idea where anything was" mother said, "So at the end of the main road we turned left, pulled into an empty parking lot of a shopping center that had a convenience store that was open all night and asked for directions. The clerk behind the counter told us about a picnic area a few miles north. It was right on the ocean and we could probably stay there until the campground opened in the morning. We pulled out of the shopping center and drove a few miles north until we saw the lights of the picnic area in the woods up ahead of us. We pulled in, drove around the small road and found us a place to park. We were exhausted and just wanted to sleep after our long ride down." My mother told me laughing, "I had to go to the bathroom bad and didn't know where the bathrooms were, I went into some bushes on the edge of the woods near where we were parked pulled my pants down and started to pee. Suddenly, a car pulls up and it was none other than a Georgia state trooper! Your father is in a panic and trying to hide the fact that I am ducking down a few feet away in the bushes using the bathroom and that I am slouching down among the palmetto bushes trying not to get my rear-end stuck by the pointy tips of the palmetto fronds." The trooper gets out of his car and says, "good evening sir", and asks "is everything ok"?

"Your father explains that he and his wife have just arrived on Jekyll after a long trip from Atlanta and planned to sleep in the truck until the campground opens in the morning. He also explains, I was out looking for the bathrooms. The trooper points out that the bathrooms are just a ways over from where we had parked. The trooper also tells us that overnight camping usually wasn't permitted in the picnic area but, since it was so late, the campground was closed and none of the motels were open; it would be okay if we slept there until morning." The trooper also said, "I'll ride by throughout the night to make sure you two are alright and that no one bothers you." "Your father thanked the trooper for his kindness as he got in his patrol car and left." After the trooper left my poor mother said, "I breathed a huge sigh of relief that I hadn't been caught as I emerged from the palmetto bushes. Your father and I both had a good laugh, got into our sleeping bags, laid down in the bed of the truck exhausted and went to sleep for the night." I enjoyed that story every time my mother told it to me and now laugh whenever I think about it. My parents first evening at the old north picnic area had started what was to be the first of many trips for my family and friends to wonderful Jekyll Island Georgia. A family tradition that has lasted for fifty-two years and is still going strong today.

CHAPTER TWO

Are we there yet?

I do not remember the first time I went to Jekyll Island, but old, black and white family photos show me as a toddler playing on the beach with my mom and the family dog. Another photo shows me in the water with my father, and yet another photo shows me on the balcony at the Jekyll Estates motel. My parents continued to go down to Jekyll after that first time after instantly falling in love with it. My father would look for any excuse to go down if only to just spend a night or two. Then as fate would have it, one of my fathers' sisters, Aunt Judy, married a United States Navy Master Chief Petty Officer named Butch Mauldin.

Uncle Butch was soon stationed at the Naval air station in Brunswick. At first they were unable to obtain base housing, and they took an apartment on Jekyll. He, Aunt Judy and their children (Gene, Trudy and Spanky) all lived in the Jekyll apartment. One my earliest memories would be of their second-floor apartment, on Captain Wylly Road right behind what is today the Lighthouse cottages. I remember they had one of those old couches that was covered in a hard plastic and was very uncomfortable to sit on. I remember that couch well because I had to sleep on it on several occasions. In a short amount of time, Uncle Butch and his family were able to get a home on the base and they moved off Jekyll. According to my mother, we never stayed with them on the base. They often spent the night with us at the campground or just for the day at the beach. Uncle Butch eventually retired from the United States Navy and moved his family from Brunswick to the Atlanta area.

Aunt Judy remarried some years later and had a son James. Jamie as he called, loved Jekyll Island as much as the rest of the family did. There is one picture of Uncle Butch and Aunt Judy with my father at the Clam Creek fishing pier. I gave that picture to my cousin Spanky shortly after Uncle Butch died a few years ago. Spanky, whose real name is Kern, received his nickname from his maternal grandmother when he was a baby. When asked Spanky had no idea why she called him that but, the name has stuck. I was born in September 1968 and my memories of Jekyll would start around age four to six, this would be 1972-74. My father Jesse was a brick mason that specialized in custom built fireplaces and ornamental brickwork and my mother Marie worked for a sub-contractor making eyeglasses and contact lenses for doctors' offices. My father loved to do things spontaneously, we would often go down to Jekyll in the middle of the night or during the day after he got home from work depending on his mood at the time. He would come home after work and announce, "pack up were going to Jekyll".

This would make my poor mother groan of course and myself just as excited as ever. I would immediately get my suitcase and start packing it. It was a brown, wooden suitcase with dark leather trim. It had a dark purple, cloth interior that reminds me even today of the interior of an old, Victorian era coffin and it had a very distinctive smell like it was riddled with moth balls

My father had an early 1970's model red, Ford pickup with a vinyl bench seat and extended bed. The truck had the gear shifter on the column and that button on the bare uncarpeted floor you mashed with your foot to brighten or dim the headlights. The radio was one of the kinds that had two big knobs, one on each end and four black push button presets in the middle with an 8-track tape player. The truck had no air conditioning, but the heat worked great in the winter. Over the extended bed, my father had a white sheet metal camper shell with louver type windows that you would crank open on both sides. There was a full glass window that was up against the cab of the truck and one to get in and out of the bed in the back. Gray carpet covered the old well-worn floor and my father had a thick piece of plywood across the back of the camper up against the cab. He could sleep on top when he was at deer camp, and it had plenty of storage space underneath.

My father got all of our camping gear out of storage and started packing the truck. Under the plywood bed, the space was packed with our Sears,

Hillary brand, canvas five-person tent; two burner Coleman stove; four lanterns; cook set; three sleeping bags; two cans of Coleman fuel; boxes of canned goods. We would add a cooler with bacon, eggs, ham, hamburger, cheese, mayo of course, my suitcase and whatever else we needed.

My parents always sat up front and I rode in the back of the truck with the back window open to check out the passing sights. I remember one trip when I was in the floor of the bed of the truck playing with my hot wheels cars when suddenly the truck swerved off the road and stopped. My mom and father came running back and were relieved to see me. They thought I had fallen out of the truck and ran back to check on me.

Now, my father absolutely hated traffic and that meant we left either late in the afternoon or very early in the morning, I am talking well before dawn. We stopped at the local gas station to fill up and I was in the back spreading out my sleeping bag on the plywood board. My thought was, "I'll sleep on the way down there and when I wake up, we'll be there." Yeah right. I laid down for a total of maybe, one minute before the excitement got to be too much for me and I was up at the back of the truck looking out the window at the rushing world fly by.

I saw many cars with suitcases and other items strapped down on top and pickup trucks with camper shells like ours on the road. Some other trucks were pulling big long travel trailers with bicycles strapped down to the rear of the trailer and others were pulling the small popup type trailers. I always wondered, where were they going, and would I see them at Jekyll or Fernandina Beach. When we would come up on a semi-truck, I would furiously start pumping my arm and fist up and down hoping the trucker would blast his airhorn and much to my excitement they often did so. We traveled down the interstate with my excitement building with each passing mile. It's funny the things you remember as a kid and how you associate road and business signs with where you're going. Around the city of Forsyth about 15 miles north of Macon there was such a sign. I was a huge Yogi Bear fan then and I remember an RV park named Yogi Bear's Jellystone RV park. It was a huge sign seen from the highway and it had Yogi's head on top of the sign. Also, in Forsyth, there was a motel right off the highway called the Tradewinds motel and a big part of the sign was a huge palm tree. I would only see that sign when we were going to Jekyll and seeing it would add to my confirmation that we were really on our way. Sadly, the RV park is no longer there, and the motel was torn down some years ago as was the sign.

Our first stop was in Macon, Georgia. We'd always got off at the Pierce Ave exit and stopped at the store at the bottom of the exit. It changed names often but, I remember it best as the Happy Store. My father would top off the gas tank and mom would always be dragging me along with her going to the bathroom. Before we left the store, I would get up front in the cab with my parents. We would get back on the highway and merge unto interstate 16 passing the Macon Coliseum where our next-door neighbor, Madge, would go hear Elvis Presley perform a few years later. We would stay on interstate 16 for a short run and it was about this area I would get my first whiff of a Sulfur smell in the air. I would get excited and ask, "Are we there yet?" They both answered, "No son, not yet."

Traveling further down interstate 16, we would get off at exit #6. I would get super excited when I saw the big green exit sign proclaim GOLDEN ISLES HWY. Excitedly, I would ask again, "Are we there yet?" "No, not yet." Getting off the exit and turning right, there was a gas station/ truck stop on the left that we always stopped at when coming home. Continuing our way, we passed private homes, churches, small grocery stores, mom and pop fruit and vegetable stands. It's funny the things that come up in a kids head and what wild imaginations they have. About six to eight miles from the exit and off in the distance, I would see these blinking lights on these tall towers and the way the roadway twisted and turned ahead of us it looked, to my young eyes like these tall towers were going to fall on us as we passed by in the truck. I would cling to my mother and hide my eyes hoping they would miss us as they fell. I learned later that they were the television transmission towers for a local Macon station WMAZ. They stood I'm guessing four hundred or more feet into the sky and were anchored to the ground by thick steel cables connected to massive concrete anchors buried deep in the ground. Passing by the towers, I'd look back feeling confident that the towers wouldn't fall on us now. Continuing our way, we passed more mom and pop gas stations, the occasional store and fruit and vegetable stands. After what seemed like hours and hours of driving, we came to our first town, the city of Cochran. We passed through the town looking at all the stores, other businesses and big stately homes. We passed a small community college that my parents told me years later some friends of theirs had a daughter that went to that school, and they helped to move her in to her dorm. There is a business on the outskirts of Cochran that I'm guessing was a grain mill of sorts but as a kid, I used to believe that I was a multi-millionaire that owned that business and I would come through town once a year to check on things and the town made a huge holiday of me arriving. I imagined the streets lined with my employees waving at me and cheering. I would just hold up one hand and wave as we drove by and they would go wild with excitement. The town band would be playing, and they would have carnival type rides all around. Passing the grain mill and leaving my imaginary business and employees behind, I settled back in the seat wondering, when will we get there?

Our next stop was the city of Eastman. In my later years especially when I would drive down by myself. I really admired Eastman and would have liked to live there one day. I called Eastman the city of ponds and lakes. They had these beautiful homes on wide pieces of land with these ponds and small lakes all over. Eastman as a small child was also a big milestone to me because, that's where we picked up Georgia highway 341. I knew when I saw that road sign, we were definitely on our way. I also knew Eastman had a Stuckey's restaurant. We would pull into the parking lot with the white building and distinctive blue roof. We would go in and immediately be hit with the wonderful smell of bacon, eggs, toast and fresh brewed coffee; but most importantly, they had those pecan rolls that I loved, My mother could not do without her pralines and my father his cigarette and cup of black coffee. Across the street, Stuckey's had a motel called Stuckey's Carriage Inn. It had a huge yellow and white sign with a horse and carriage on it and with yellow pyramid shapes on the top. I faintly remember seeing this same sign on Jekyll and of course asked, "Are we there yet?" "No!!", came back the answer.

We passed through the next towns of Helena and McRae, it was here that I saw my first Piggly Wiggly grocery store and thought that was a funny name for a store. Going through these small towns, I saw certain products and businesses that I'd never heard of before and were only available in South Georgia. A few of these were Merita Bread, Pet milk and ice cream, Lance crackers and snacks, Captain Joe's seafood, and Stuckey's. There were also Bay gas stations in some of the towns we passed through as well as Zippy Mart convenience stores. I'm not sure which gas station it was but, I was old enough to go to the restroom by myself. When I walked inside, I saw on the wall, there was a white cloth towel that spun around inside of a white metal type box on a loop. When you pulled on the towel if you found a clean enough spot, which were few and far between, you dried your hands on it. The cloth towel was heavily soiled and filthy, and I was still young enough to not care about germs. Today, I imagine my mother would be horrified if she had seen what I dried my hands on. When I was a little older, I'd say around eleven or twelve we stopped at a service station in the town of Baxley, I saw this machine on the wall in the bathroom that dispensed what looked like colorful balloons. I managed to get the two quarters put together to put in the machine and out came my balloon. It was green not my favorite color, and it had a weird shape, but it would do. After I got back in the car, I got the balloon out of the package and tried to blow it up. My mother looked at what I was doing and saw the shape of my balloon and started to panic. She asked in a trembling voice, "Where did you get that, or did you pick that up off the ground?" I replied, "No, I got it out of a machine in the bathroom."

She immediately calmed down. I got my first lesson about birth control and what that green balloon was really for. At that time, I knew enough about sex to know that's how babies were made but not about condoms and how and why they were used.

The local Dairy Queen in McRae was one of our stops when we went down in the daylight hours. I remember they always had a spiritual Christian message that I would look forward to seeing on the sign out front that said, *Jesus Loves you* on one side and *God Loves you* on the other. Passing through recently, I was glad to see they still posted those messages after all this time. Then it was on to Hazlehurst. As a child, Hazlehurst didn't have much to hold a child's imagination but in my later childhood and early teen years, it did. Mainly what captured my attention was their local radio station WVOH. I remember going through Hazlehurst after my parents divorced. I was twelve and with my mother driving, I would be trying to find a radio station. Anyone that's been on a trip back in the 1960's thru the 80's, well before satellite radio came along then knows the pain of finding a good station with great music only to lose it a few miles later and then spend the next five or ten minutes trying find another one. We found WVOH 93.5 on the dial one day passing through Hazlehurst early in the morning and they were telling the local news including the schools lunch menus and surprisingly the local schools absentee list of all students that day. I remarked to my mother, "I hope we never move here, I could never lay out of school without you finding out." She laughed and said smiling, "maybe we should move here." They also announced people's birthdays and wedding anniversaries. The station had a host that had a very distinctive voice that announced local events and commercials. I liked the small town feel of the radio station. The station also carried national and world news through the USA radio network news organization which I later made it a habit of listening to on my computer at home. We later made Hazlehurst a regular stop in the morning because of a great restaurant called Corursen's County Kitchen now called Papa's Cabin. They had a great breakfast buffet with bacon, eggs, sausage, hash browns, grits biscuits with gravy and the best sweet tea around. This place was always busy, especially during deer season. Leaving Hazlehurst, WVOH would soon fade out and the search was on for a new station.

We would pass through other towns like Lumber city with their iconic turntable Railroad bridge that spanned the Ocmulgee river and a motel that had the greenest pool I have ever seen. The pool wasn't dirty, it was just painted that way. That place was always full.

Our next town was Baxley Georgia. I would get very excited here, because I would see my first palm trees and road signs pointing the way to Brunswick. There was also a gas station that had blue tinted windows just like the windows of the Jekyll Pharmacy. "Are we there yet?" "No!! not yet."

On the outskirts of Baxley there is a wood processing plant that processed logs into boards and produced other wood products. Along the road they would have these huge towering piles of logs at least fifty feet tall with water sprinklers keeping them wet and sheds full of finished wood products. At night, they had huge flood lights almost like stadium lights that would light up the whole yard and it made the piles of logs seem that much larger. Passed there is Captain Joe's seafood restaurant. Right behind there is the site of an old Drive-in movie.

As a kid we passed there one evening in the late 1970's and they were playing *Rocky II*. I remember the scene too, Rocky and Mickey were in the hospital chapel waiting on Adrian to recover from a coma after giving birth to Rocky junior and Mickey is trying to persuade Rocky not to blow his second chance at a shot at the title. I jumped up and down in the back of the truck all excited and punching my fists in the air like a boxer. I really loved that movie.

Outside the town of Baxley, this section of Georgia highway 341 is the flattest stretch of roadway I've ever been on. Between Baxley and the next town of Surrency is ten miles of completely flat road. As a young child, I remembered my mother remarked on how she could see the blinking amber traffic light at an intersection in Surrency in the middle of the night ten miles away. We would see that light and wonder would we ever get to it. That light is still there to this day and that stretch of highway 341 is still the flattest I have been on. During the heat of the day, you can see the waves of heat coming off of the pavement and the cars approaching you from the other side look like ghosts coming up out of the road. It reminds me of the opening scene of the Clint Eastwood movie *High Plains Drifter*.

Our next town would be Jesup I would be seeing a lot more palm trees and more road signs to Brunswick. In Jesup there was a building that had a high-pitched roof that was striped like a candy cane. The sign read Towel and Tog shop. Mom said that they sold towels in there. I thought it was a candy store, so my interest quickly died there.

My grandparents Luther and Mildred Johnson went with my mom and I to Jekyll in the summer of 1981. When we came through Jesup, we came up to some railroad tracks just as we were crossing over, the traffic light changes to red and we're stuck right in the middle of the tracks. While waiting on the light to change, the red lights start to flash, and the bell starts clanging. I yell out, "A train is coming!" As my poor mom is trying to get over the tracks the railroad crossing arm comes down and hits the trunk of the car with a big THUD. We pull on over the tracks with the crossing arm scraping and bouncing across the trunk of the car. We get safely over to the other side and the train with its horn blaring, passes us safely by. For years after that day whenever we pass through Jesup, I would jokingly give my poor mom a hard time about that crossing.

One night in the mid 1970's a few miles outside of Jesup, we ran through a swarm of mosquitoes, gnats and other bugs that peppered the windshield of the old pickup truck so bad we could hardly see out of it. My father instinctively turns on the windshield wipers and makes the situation even worse. Cursing, he then pulls over on the side of the road, grabs two cans of Coca Cola out of the cooler in back of the truck and pours them on the windshield. He lets it set for a few moments and turns the wipers back on. The combination of carbonation and acid cleans the windshield enough so we can see out of it. We continued on our way through miles and miles of lonely country road with thick pine forests on both sides dotted with logging roads cut into them and fire watch towers standing vigil over the forest that lay below them. We passed through smaller towns named Graham, Pine Grove, Odum, Everett, Sterling and Gardi. Finally, after what seemed like an eternity, I saw the sign that said Brunswick City limits. My poor parents would then say with pleasure, "Hey Son, were finally here."

Once we arrived in Brunswick, we pulled into one of the few gas stations open at that late hour and while my mother is filling up the gas tank, my father grabs a garden hose and squeegee and washed the rest of the sticky coca cola off the windshield, hood and the fenders. The rest of the poor truck looked like it had been peppered with shotgun pellets. He washes it off the truck as best as he could, and we continued on our way.

CHAPTER THREE

Finally here

As a child, and still to this day, I always focused on signs. Which signs changed and which ones stayed the same served as landmarks on our many trips to Jekyll. On Georgia highway 42/23, not far from my old house in Forest Park and just before you arrived in the city of Stockbridge, there was a small billboard for Jekyll Island that was hidden by the overgrown trees and brush. I imagine this billboard was put up because before the interstate system was built, highway 42 was one of the few roads that led to Macon and coastal Georgia. In Brunswick, street signs have pretty much stayed the same as have a lot of the businesses. I've always wanted a street sign so I could have a piece of Brunswick to take home with me. A few years ago, I even went as far as having an official Brunswick city limit sign made and tried trading with the city for one of their old ones so I could hang in my garage. Unfortunately, they had already changed signs and had the new ones up. The one I had made is in my garage now.

In those early years, finally arriving in Brunswick, my little eyes darted all around trying not to miss a thing. We drove under interstate 95 going towards downtown Brunswick. Driving by gas stations, used car lots, the ever-present Waffle House, and the biggest cemetery I've ever seen. That cemetery was right by the city's water treatment plant and seemed to go on forever.

The sulfur smell I associated the coastal area was the strongest here. I could see the smokestack of the Hercules plant billowing out huge amounts of, I guessed steam, looking like a never-ending stream of cotton flowing into the sky. Once we left the downtown area and into the residential area at night the streetlights would cast strange spooky shadows through the Spanish moss that hung everywhere like curtains off the century old oak trees. I remember best the winding road that took us through the residential areas right turn here, left turn there and so forth. Going down Newcastle street, we would drive by warehouses and the adjoining rail lines that serviced the state docks. Then by the International Seamans house and the entrance to the state docks on the right and turning left unto fourth avenue, a tree lined street with old established homes on either side. Over the railroad tracks on the right was a business, Golden Isles Building Supply. Past that we reached the end of Highway 341/Fourth Avenue. At the intersection of fourth avenue and Georgia highway 17 you could look out past the roadway and across the marsh on the left to see St. Simons island with its iconic lighthouse flickering in the distance, and of course, Jekyll Island with a few flickering lights on the right. Turning right onto highway 17, my excitement was at a fever pitch.

We went down the road and around a curve past the sign to the Coast Guard station on the left. A huge warehouse sat on the right with the name B/W on a world globe. Babcock and Wilcox were boiler makers that moved into the Warehouse after World War 2. I found out only recently what B/W stood for. I watched a PBS special on World War 2's impact on coastal Georgia and Brunswick. The Warehouse was part of the shipyard that built the liberty ships so vital to the war effort. Passing the warehouse, we were heading for what I called the big bridge. The big bridge loomed up out of the darkness with red aircraft warning beacons blinking on tops of each of the four towers. The bridge was called The Sidney Lanier bridge. It was built in 1956 and was the site I later learned of a tragic collision when it was hit by a ship in November of 1972 and a few non-fatal collisions could come after that. I could hear and feel the thump thump, thump thump, thump thump as the old Ford pickup was on the approach span.

Up ahead was a traffic signal showing a steady green, and at night, the light cast an eerie glow on the roadway below. Just right after we moved out of the light I heard a sound I have been waiting to hear all day or all night. Drrrrrrrrrrrrrrrrr the sound the truck tires made as we rode over the grate of the lift span and then, thump thump, thump thump, thump thump as we rode down the southern span.

At the end of the span, was a sign Jekyll Island next left. We made a left and approached the Entrance towers with a red and blue sign strung between the two towers JEKYLL ISLAND YEAR AROUND BEACH RESORT. In later years we always stopped at the towers to take a picture and even to this day my wife Kathy and I stop to take photos of the new entrance with the beautiful ponds. At night the causeway was very eerie and quite because some sections were totally dark and then a lone light pole with an amber colored light surrounded with hundreds of mosquitoes shined down on the road.

One thing fascinated me on the causeway, that was the power poles buried in the marsh along side the road. There were two poles spaced apart about eight feet and they had an X bracing between them. To me they looked funny and yes, I have taken plenty of pictures of these poles. On the left we would pass by the Liquor store that my father frequently visited on our trips. Later it was a Shell gas station and today is the welcome center with Georgia State Patrol offices. After a slight curve in the road, we approached the Jekyll river bridge. It too stood majestically there, it also had aircraft warning beacons on its two towers and a traffic signal with a steady green that cast that same eerie glow on the roadway at night. Thump thump, thump thump and then drrrrrrrr then thump thump, thump thump. We were finally here!!!

Once you cross the Jekyll river bridge onto Jekyll Island, time seems to slow down. I always had the feeling that we passed through a time warp to another era. People seem to smile more, be nicer, more considerate, and less in a hurry.

My wife, Kathy and I had arrived for the summer of 2017 and were having lunch at Red Bug pizza. There was a Future Farmers of America meeting going on at the same time and we sat next to the nicest, most considerate group of teenagers from the northern part of Georgia. We also encountered many college students at the yogurt shop, ordinary people in the new beach village and others all throughout the island whom were just as friendly as ever. Jekyll brings out the best in people. In my 49 plus years of going to Jekyll Island, I have never felt unsafe, uneasy or had a bad experience of any kind, except the time I lost my truck keys and had to call a locksmith to make a new set, or the time one of my Uncle's and I got caught by the fast rising tide on the new Jekyll sandbar. You'll read about later. Before the automated toll booth that is now operating at the welcome center was operational, they had a small toll booth that looked like a small beach house at the bottom of the hill as you drove onto Jekyll. You'd pull up in the pay line and a friendly older woman or gentleman would greet you at all hours of the day or night, take your two dollars and hand it off to a person inside the booth. Then they'd hand you a map of Jekyll with all the latest information and goings on printed on it. The cars with annual passes or extended passes would drive by on the far right and they would just wave them on through. After you received your brochure and receipt, you would continue on your way.

Driving down the Ben Fortson parkway it was dark and very quiet except with the occasional streetlight with its soft amber glow filling up the street and surrounding area. We passed the Phillips 66 service station on the left, where over the years we've had a few tires patched up from sharp bits of shells and the occasional nail or screw. At the end of the parkway, at intersection of Ben Fortson parkway and Beach View drive, we turned left and pulled in the darken and deserted parking lot of the island's shopping center. The only store open at that late hour was the Zippy Mart convenience store. As I said at the beginning of this chapter, I had a thing about signs. The Zippy Mart sign reminded me of the color on the package of a pack of Nutter Butter peanut butter sandwich cookies.

Stepping inside the store, it was the normal sights, sounds and smells of a convenience store. The freezer with the hand dipped ice cream humming away, the squeak of the carousel turning the hot dogs under the hot lamps, the smell of stale popcorn, the coolers with every imaginable soft drink and juice available, a magazine rack with the latest magazines and, of course my favorite, the candy isle. On the counter was the cash register and big glass jars of pickled eggs, pickled pigs' feet and pickled sausages. My father always had to pick up some smokes, my mom a drink and me a candy bar. One night after we arrived, my mother and I were outside, and my father was still inside. I looked around the dark parking lot and over on the edge of the lot beside the Jekyll Island seafood house restaurant stood a lone phone both. Its white fluorescent bulb was flashing like a strobe light with what seemed like a thousand gnats and mosquitoes dancing all around it.

I walked up to the booth and there was buzzing kind of loud. I pushed the door open and reached up to the metal self that held the well-worn phonebook attached by a metal cable and touched it. I got quite a shock, not enough to hurt but enough to scare me more than it hurt. I ran back to the truck where my mother was at and waited on my father to come out. Pulling out of the parking lot, we passed the convention center and swimming pool on the right and then a wide expanse of paved parking lot that would one day become the Great Dunes park. We passed the darken miniature golf area, a restaurant up on a hill that was Mulligans Sandwich shop. Mulligan's later became Black Beards restaurant and now is Tortuga Jacks a baja Mexican restaurant. Continuing on down Beachview drive, in the daytime, we would have a spectacular unobstructed view of the Atlantic Ocean and then the road took a slight curve, and we would see the Wanderer motel on the right and the Seafarer on the left. Further down was the Jekyll Estates motel. We passed some homes that in the daytime you could see were painted in teal green and salmon pink colors with concrete lattice type walls on the outside and around the carport. Then we passed the Sand Dollar apartments that would later become the Jekyll Inn, and now is a development of new homes. We also passed an area of maritime forest with a carpet of palmetto bushes that would one day become the Villas by the sea. In this area up in the distance you could see a little light shining in the woods. This was the entrance to the North Picnic area now it is called Driftwood Beach. In the daytime coming down this road, the tree canopy covering the forest on both sides of the road was flat except for a lone tree standing taller than anything else. This lone tree marked like a beacon to where the picnic area was. We pulled into the picnic area just before midnight and found us a spot. We got out of the truck and walked up to the spot to where the beach crossover went over the Johnson rocks and out onto the wide beach. We looked out into the stark blackness, the ocean breeze blowing in your face felt so refreshing. The tide was out because the sounds of the waves were distant and offshore you could see the red and green lights on the navigation buoys that marked the entrance to the shipping channel flashing in the night. Looking up into the sky, you could see what seemed like millions of stars against a ink black sky. To the left you could see the lighthouse on Saint Simons Island streaming its light out into the darkness warning ships of the many sandbars in the area and welcoming ships from around the world to the port of Brunswick. Looking back through the picnic area, under the soft amber glow of strategically placed streetlights, we could see the bathrooms and countless concrete picnic tables with metal grills mounted in the ground standing all about. The Spanish moss hanging from the gnarly wind-swept trees cast weird shadows all about. Overnight parking was apparently allowed then because we were never asked to leave. We pulled out our sleeping bags and tried to sleep while waiting for the campgrounds to open in the morning but, it was no use. The excitement of finally being here, and what was to come, kept you awake until, the humming of the amber colored streetlights and the crashing of the not too distance ocean waves finally put you to sleep.

CHAPTER FOUR

A day on Jekyll

My father was always an early riser and had no patience whatsoever; that meant we all were early risers if we liked it or not. I remember many Christmases as a child where I would be woken up well before or shortly after midnight on Christmas Eve because my father couldn't wait until morning for me to open my presents. After a good night's sleep, I would wake up and at first think I am still at home in bed and then after a few moments I would get so excited because I knew then where I was. I would get up, get out of my sleeping bag, throw on my shorts and shoes then crawl out of the back of the truck. Mom would be sitting in her chair enjoying the quiet morning with her coffee and my father would be on the beach feeding Cheezit crackers a dozen or more sea gulls. I have a picture that my Mom took of my father feeding the sea gulls early one morning. As soon as my father returned from feeding the gulls, we rolled up our bags, jumped in the truck and headed to the campground. Other people began arriving to enjoy the day at the beach too. Arriving at the Cherokee campground on the northern most end of the island, you would see a large wooden sign with an Indian head on top and wooden panels below announcing the services they provided: groceries, white gas, (which is another name for unleaded gas), hot showers, camping supplies, tackle and bait etc. We pulled in under the canopy of trees that covered the entire campground in year around shade. Stopping at the camp store to register, I saw racks of bikes belonging to other campers and ones they had for rent. You could hear birds of all kinds singing and chirping in the trees; and the squirrels would be running around eating nuts or whatever someone had dropped on the ground.

Beside the rusted ice machine under an awning there were signs for Pet milk and Merita Bread. Beside them were the R C, Coca Cola, and Pepsi drink machines along with a Lance cracker and other snack machines. Stepping inside through the heavy wooden door, the camp store had the convenience store smell. Large coolers that lined the back wall held all varieties of food and drinks. A lone cooler in the corner that looked like an ice cream cooler, held shrimp, fish and chicken that was used as bait. Among the isles in the center of the room were canned goods, bread, Coleman fuel, lantern mantels, tackle, rods and reels, beach toys, t-shirts, laundry detergent, bar soap and various other dry goods. At the counter as my father was registering us in, I was checking out the brochure rack by the door.

With our campsite number in hand we headed out. Leaving the store, we passed by travel trailers, popup campers, and the big motor homes all with their awnings out; tables and chairs setup; grills standing by to work; beach towels hanging up to dry; bikes parked and pets running around. We reached our campsite and started to setup. Out would come the big Sears Hillary canvas tent. It would be spread out and stakes driven in and then the song of clanging and banging of tent poles trying to figure out what went where. Finally, it was up, I'd step inside to unzip the window flaps to air it out. The inside of the tent was already hot and musty but felt better once a breeze came through. The dark and white sand mixed with those small leaves already all over the place and mom fighting the never-ending battle of keeping the inside of the tent swept out with an old well-used corn broom. The sleeping bags and pillows were laid out along with my old suitcase. The kitchen was setup next. The Coleman stove along with the cook set and utensils were setup on a small table and my father would fill the lanterns for that evening. The cooler and boxes of dry goods were setup by the old wood and metal picnic table. Breakfast would be next; the old Coleman stove was fired up. The smell of our breakfast soon filled the air and was mixed in with our neighbor's campfires. The smell of burning Coleman fuel just smelled heavenly. After breakfast we'd get ready to head back to the beach. We had a smaller cooler that held drinks, bread, sandwich meat, and mayonnaise that went with us. We'd throw on our blue jean cutoffs, grab our towels, and the cooler then jump in the truck to head back to the Old North picnic area.

Arriving back, it was busier than when we left. We pulled up to a spot just in front of the Johnson rocks, by the crossover, just under the famous tree that stood taller than all the others and claimed our spot. Looking out over the wide beach, the breeze was stronger than before but felt just as fresh. You could no longer see the navigation buoys in the distance as we did last night, but there were a few shrimp boats in the distance with their nets in the water. Looking over towards Saint Simons Island, you could see the lighthouse along with countless homes and buildings in the distance. We staked out our spot on the beach among other beach goers with umbrellas, towels, and coolers. I remember the air being filled with the smell of Copper Tone suntan lotion. In 1972 the transistor radios on the beach and in the picnic area played the popular song *Witchy Woman* by the Eagles numerous times. We would be out on the beach for quite a while enjoying ourselves playing in the water and seeing an occasional ship passing by on its way to Brunswick or elsewhere.

I remember one day on the beach; we had been in the water enjoying ourselves for quite some time. We got back on the beach, couldn't find our spot and swore someone had robbed us of our towels, shoes, and the old 126 Kodak camera. Come to find out, it was extremely breezy that day and the sand had covered everything up. Luckily, we found our stuff, but our poor camera had some major sand damage. With a little luck and some diligent cleaning, the camera was saved along with the film inside. For years after that, that poor camera had flakes of sand in the viewfinder and on the lense. We were unable to get all of the sand out but, it still took great pictures until one day it finally gave up the ghost. At lunch we headed back to our table under the shade of the trees to eat. We usually had drinks with bread, ham, turkey, bologna and potted meat; with potato chips and cookies. Sitting around the picnic table after lunch resting you could see what everyone else was doing. Various other types of vehicles were parked everywhere, towels and bathing suits hung everywhere to dry out; grills were fired up cooking burgers, steaks and chicken. With the smoke hanging low over the area the smell of it all mixed in with the salt air and just made it smell that much better.

One day we met a young couple with two children about my age and they were frying porkchops and shrimp in a cast iron skillet on one of the many grills in the picnic area and invited us to eat with them. My father of course supplied the beer. I believe it was the first time I had ever ate sunbeam bread. I remember it so well because it was small and tore very easily. It wasn't easy making a porkchop and shrimp sandwich out of that bread but, it was still good.

Late in the afternoon we'd head back to the campground to get washed up and rest before dinner. We usually had hamburgers and baked beans that first night and they were good. Mom would be doing the burgers and I would help my father with the lanterns. I would try to pump the little piston on the side of the lanterns to pressurize the fuel but, I barely got a push and a half in before my thumbs hurt, and I gave up. My father would strike a match and stick it up inside the glass globe to light the mantels. They would flame up and consume the mantels and fire would pour out of the top of the lantern through the vents. After my father adjusted the fuel gauge, the flames died down and the mantels glowed brightly with a slight roar. The smell of the Coleman fuel burning in those lanterns was one of smells I remember the most. The moths and mosquitoes soon found the lanterns and they began their nightly dance around the hot globes.

We would then gather wood for a fire. Once it was lit and going, we all sat around talking, and my father played his harmonica. Uncle Butch and his family sometimes joined us. We would go out to find the perfect stick; roast marshmallows; and have a great evening laughing and telling funny jokes or ghost stories, like the escaped murderer with a hook for a hand. The fire would be burning brightly, and the smell of the wood burning was just wonderful. To this day, if I smell a campfire, it instantly takes me back to those evenings at Cherokee Campground.

I remember one night I may have been about six or seven years old, my father sent me to the camp store for something, not sure what it was. The campground was filled to capacity that evening and I walked through the area looking at everyone at their campsites enjoying the night. I passed by campers that had colorful lights much like Christmas lights hanging from their awnings and people sitting around talking and laughing. Some were eating dinner, and some were watching tv outside. I passed by this one large camper trailer and everyone was outside seated in lawn chairs around an old tv. Low and behold, they were watching my favorite tv show ever *Emergency*. I stopped dead in my tracks and started watching with them. They had no idea I was behind them watching until this big hand fell on my little shoulder. It was my father. He said, "Where have you been? Your mother and I were worried."

I stammered about and said, "I was heading to the store and wanted to watch *Emergency*." My father laughed, the people turned around, my father explained what I was doing, and they all laughed. They offered to let me watch the show with them and would make sure I got back okay but, my father said, "that's alright, he's already seen this episode". This was in the day where you could do something like that and trust people without worry. As I said earlier, Jekyll Island brings out the best in people. Disappointed, I headed on to the store with my father and back to our campsite to bed down for the night.

The next day we traveled to the southside to Saint Andrews Beach to spend the day. Before the conservation efforts of today, you could basically pull right up next to the beach and park right in the area of where the ramp and boardwalk are now at. There was a big pavilion in the middle of what is now the parking lot and it had lots of picnic tables and grills full of hamburgers, hot dogs, chicken, steaks, and pork chops and the smell mixed with the salt air just made it smell even better We would spend all day at this beach as well and shell hunting was better too. Uncle Butch, Aunt Judy, Gene, Trudy, and Spanky would always meet us at the campground. They came from the Naval base to spend the day and sometimes the night with us.

There were no waves here to speak of because the area was protected by the river itself and surrounding marsh from the full onslaught of the ocean. They were small waves almost like ripples and they carved and contoured the mud and sand like rumble strips on a roadway that would play havoc on one's feet. Further up the beach there was an area that had a bunch of old oyster shells and I remember one day, this kid that was more than a few years younger than myself had gashed his foot open walking around the oyster shells. His father was carrying him back to one of the picnic tables in the pavilion and this poor kid was crying and bleeding bad, soon the ambulance arrived and took him to the hospital. After that, I was warned by my father not to go around the oyster shells without shoes. Just right off the beach in the water was a green navigation light that flashed every five seconds or so. It looked like it was so close but, when you were swimming to it, it felt like forever. I would always turn back to the beach.

One time we were at St. Andrews, and I was about ten years old, there was a shrimp boat that had beached itself. The name of the boat was the *Scalper* It was cool to walk around and see what a shrimp boat looked like out of the water and how big the propellers were. We never did find out why the boat was beached but, she was gone by the next day. My mother, father and I were walking along the shore on St. Andrews one night. My father was carrying a lantern and I had a flashlight. I was shining the light in the water as it softly rippled to shore. Suddenly, this blue crab comes up and starts chasing me and my light. I'm running down the beach screaming and crying because this crab is after me. I dropped the flashlight and run behind my parents for protection; the crab leaves me alone. My mother and father had a great laugh over that.

The biggest thing I loved to watch at St. Andrews, was when people would be out seine fishing. Seine fishing is when two people use long a net, I'd say about three feet wide and ten feet long and the net would hang vertical with weights on the bottom and floats on the top. I would watch as the person on the far end would be out in the water up to their neck dragging the net along the bottom in a wide arc and making their way back to shore. Once on shore, we'd all go and look at what they brought in. it would be the usual fish, shrimp, flounder, blue crabs, baby sharks and the occasional shells.

On the way back to the campground, we would, as my mother would say, "go visit the Horton's." We would stop by the Horton House, walk around the ruins of the house, look at the cemetery and look out over the marsh towards Brunswick. We would go visit the Calm Creek fishing pier at both day and night. During the day my father would spend a lot of time here fishing and I even tried my hand a crabbing with not too much success. Again, before the preservation efforts, you could park right up next to the pier entrance and basically anywhere you wanted. There was no fishing store, just a bathroom situated among the many concrete picnic tables and grills. The pier would be packed on certain days as would the beach area below the pier. The little bridge over Clam Creek just to the right of the pier was a favorite spot for fishing also. The powerline hanging just behind the bridge was always covered in lost fishing line, floats and lures.

I liked going to the pier at night because that was when the shark fishermen were out there. Pulling up at night, it was eerie looking. The amber lights just like at the north picnic area shown through the trees and Spanish moss casting those weird and creepy shadows. Amber lights lined the pier, shining brightly and the mosquitoes and moths are performing their dance. There was a small snack bar on the pier that sold soft drinks and snacks. There were bathrooms on the pier as well. The snack bar and bathrooms were torn down years ago but, you can still see the small blue and white tile floor on the pier deck today. We would make it to where the shark fishermen were at. Their rods were as big as my little arm and their reels as big as a car steering wheel. When they got a bite, the fishermen would start cranking his reel furiously and I would hear that distinctive click, click, click sound I remember hearing on the movie 'Jaws' years later. They had caught sharks earlier and had the meat in big coolers on ice and the jaws were laid out to dry on the blood-stained pier deck. At certain points along the pier, there were big white lights mounted just under where you stood shining down in the green water swirling around the shell and clam encrusted pilings. I would stare down at the water and remember thinking, that water must be hundreds of feet deep.

We got great closeup views of the many ships going in and out of the port of Brunswick. As the ships passed, they would stir up some big waves that you could watch coming in and start crashing into the pilings and shore. We would lean on the railings and feel the breeze blowing in our face and look out across the water at the lights from Brunswick flickering in the distance. I could see the aircraft warning lights on the big bridge as I called it blinking in the distance and you could barely make out the headlights of various vehicles on the bridge.

We would head back to our campsite traveling down the winding dark road from the pier to the end and then across the street to the campground. The camp sign shining brightly for all to see and the camp store closed for the night. The yellow colored fluorescent bulbs luminating the drink and snack machines outside of the store reminded me of the lights at a traveling carnival. Before going to bed, I had to take a shower to wash the sand out of my britches. As all young kids, I hated taking a bath let alone a shower. My mom would take me with her to the bathhouse. It was a cinder block building painted brown and white with a concrete lattice type wall on the outside with yellow fluorescent bulbs casting their glow on everything. Stepping over the ever-present water puddle just outside the door, I'd step inside. The floors were always wet, it smelled musty. The ever-present sand and small leaves were everywhere. There was a sign posted on the wall inside, "Do not wash dishes in bathhouse" I would reluctantly take my shower in the sulfur water or the smelly egg water as I called it and waited on mom to take hers. When we finished, we would make our way back through the much quieter campground, everyone having moved inside their trailers and tents for the evening.

When we made it back to our site and my father would be sitting by the campfire softly playing *Blue eyes crying in the rain* on his harmonica. I would sit beside him for a while listening, humming along as he played and listening to the campfire snapping and crackling as it slowly consumed the wood and watching the white smoke that helped to keep the bugs away rising into the air and disappearing into the night sky. Soon, my eyes start to get heavy and I make my way to the tent. As I step inside and slip into my sleeping bag to go to sleep for the night, my mom tucks me in and kisses me good night. As my head slowly sinks into my pillow, I lay there listening to the roar of the Coleman lantern that sits just outside the tent, the sound of the lantern is nearly drowned out by what seems like millions of crickets and frogs chirping and croaking all around us. My eyes are slowing closing now and I finally drift off to sleep. The next morning, I am the first one up and as I step outside the tent, the sounds of the crickets and frogs have been replaced by the many birds that call Jekyll home. The Lantern that was roaring when I fell asleep is now at its dimmest and almost out of fuel. I grab some orange juice out of the cooler and pour me some in a white Styrofoam cup and sit at the picnic table and read a book that mom bought for me at the camp store called *The Animal Fair*. I wait for my parents to wake up to start another great day on Jekyll Island

The Author age 2 and his Mother with the family
dog at the North Picnic area Beach: 1970
Note: St. Simons Lighthouse can be seen in the distance.
Author's collection

The Author age 2 and his Mother at the North Picnic area Beach: 1970
This area was to later become Driftwood Beach.
Author's collection

The Author age 2 outside the Jekyll Estates Motel: 1970
Author's collection

One of the power poles on the Jekyll Causeway with the X
bracing that so fascinated the Author as a child: 1978
The power poles installed during the 1960's, are
currently being replaced with concrete poles.
Author's collection

The camp store at The Jekyll Island Campground
formally known as Cherokee Campground: 2005
Where the ice machines are located is where the Lance snack machines,
and RC Cola machines stood under yellow fluorescent lights.
Author's collection

The Wanderer Motel as seen from the swimming
pool of the Seafarer Motel: 1970
Photo Credit: Gerald Strickland
Reprinted with permission

Picnicking at the Cherokee Campground: 1973
From left: Cousin Trudy, Aunt Judy, Author's Mother, Cousin Gene.
Author's collection

The fishing vessel scalper beached at St. Andrews Beach: 1978
Author's collection

The Author age 4 on the docks at the historic Jekyll Wharf: 1973
Shrimp boats were allowed to tie up and sell their
catch right off of the docks at that time.
Author's collection

CHAPTER FIVE

The later years on Jekyll

My Aunt Ginny joined my mother and I down at Jekyll during the summer of 1980. I had turned 12 years old and remember that year well because the entire southeastern United States was in the grips of a severe heat wave. Temperatures that summer reached into the mid to high 90's with a lot of days at 100 degrees or above and with little or no rain for weeks on end. This trip marked one of the few times when we didn't drive our usual route. We had always heard about the Okefenokee Swamp but had never visited it. After arriving in the town of Baxley, we took the highway south and arrived in Waycross just after lunch. When we arrived at the park, it was a hot and blistering day. We went inside the gift shop to get some relief from the heat and to get our tickets for the swamp boat ride. We were told the tours were cancelled because the part of the swamp that they would take you on for the tour had dried up from the severe heat and lack of rain. Sure enough when we walked outside, the boats were sitting high and dry in the hard-cracked heat baked mud of the swamp.

We walked around the compound and saw the animals they had on display such as, birds, snakes, deer and of course alligators. Years later I went back to the Okefenokee and took that swamp boat ride. It was fascinating. The swamp water was the color of the sweet, iced tea that I love to drink and seeing alligators, snakes, birds and other wildlife in their natural habitat and not behind cages or fences was great. We left Waycross and headed to Jekyll. I discovered something else on that trip, the X bracing between two power poles that I spoke about earlier was not an exclusive thing to the Jekyll causeway. I saw them for quite a few miles on Highway 520 before we arrived at I 95 and highway 17. Once we arrived on Jekyll, the heat was intense everywhere on the island except the beach area. I believe I remember that it hadn't rained in so long that all campfires at the campground and elsewhere on the island were banned until further notice. We did spend a lot of time at the beach or the swimming pool on that trip.

My Aunt Ginny and Uncle Henry went to Jekyll with mom and I a few years later. My Aunt Ginny had this little Miata car and I was amazed that she and Uncle Henry traveled all that way in that little car. I always joked that you didn't sit in the car, you had to put it on like a glove. We had a great time that year. One bright and sunny day we were all at the Jekyll Island Club's beach pavilion, and the famous Jekyll sandbar had just begun to make one its first appearances. People were way out on the sand bar maybe two hundred yards. Uncle Henry and I decided to go out and join them. We reached the end and the tide was coming back in fast! We hurriedly made our way back to the beach not before we were up to our chests in the fast-rising water. We later counted ourselves very lucky that day. We heard later that summer and in later years that some people weren't so lucky and had drowned. The Jekyll fire department started stationing personnel on the beach during low tide to watch for anyone in trouble. I never went back out on the sandbar after that and now they have warning signs posted about the dangers of the shifting sandbar and fast rising water.

Mom and I took a sunset cruise one afternoon back in the early 1990's. The boat was called the *Tradewinds II* and was docked at the historic wharf. It was about 30 feet long with a wheelhouse forward toward the bow and plenty of seating and places to stand at the stern. This tour lasted almost two hours and was 15.00 and well worth the money. We sailed up the Jekyll river towards St. Simons Sound. The narrator on the boat was a very knowledgeable man that knew a lot about the history of Jekyll and the eco-system of the surrounding marsh. We sailed north getting a perspective few people get. We sailed passed the airport, the Horton house and a dangerous, well-marked, jetty with choppy surf splashing over the rocks that were showing just above the water at the mouth of the Jekyll river. Sailing passed the jetties; we made our way out into the open water of the bay. We sailed past the busy Calm Creek pier with everyone out fishing or sightseeing. We then turned into St. Simons sound leaving the protected waters of the inner bay and the water got rougher. The captain turned the boat broadside against the waves for a few moments, so we could really feel the rolling of the boat. We chugged on passed the lighthouse and a green can buoy that marked the demarcation line. This was the end of the State of Georgia's territorial limit and start of federal waters. We floated around awhile and enjoyed the sights. We sailed passed St. Simons light and the pier which was busier than the Clam Creek pier. People on the pier waving at us and we all waved back enthusiastically. Heading back, the sun began setting providing us with a beautiful sunset. We passed the jetty now completely uncovered due to the receding tide, the warning buoy flashing at the mouth of the Jekyll river and the airport with the runway all lit up for nighttime landings. We come up to the dock. The captain expertly slides his boat into his slip and the boats hands tie us off. We all began to disembark and go back to our vehicles. It is now completely dark, but the Jekyll Island club hotel is all lit up. The iconic tower with its blue and white pennant flying proudly acted as a beacon to all around. Everyone on the boat had now gone their separate ways but, we soon realized all had one thing in mind. These were the days before the Dairy Queen had arrived and a lot of us ended up at the Zippy Mart convenience store standing in a long line for hand dipped ice cream. While in line, we encounter a lot of people we met on the boat and we all start talking about each other's favorite part of the cruise. We stand there talking, and more and more people arrive until the line is out the door. With our ice cream in hand, we all go our separate ways to continue our Jekyll vacations.

In 1991 I took a childhood friend of mine Mike Martin with me to Jekyll; Mike and I arrived early one morning and were unable to check in. The old north picnic area had been closed to vehicle traffic at that time, beach erosion had begun a few years earlier and started claiming the trees closest to the Johnson rocks. Mike and I walked through the area with my camcorder and I started videoing. It was sad that this place where I had so many memories was disappearing but, it now has a new life as Driftwood Beach. Many of those old, gnarly, wind twisted, trees that provided shade to countess beach goers over the years are now the focus of many family photo sessions, weddings, and even star in hit TV shows, or music videos.

We decided to park at St. Andrews picnic area and slept for a few hours. Later that day, after checking in at the Jekyll Estates, we went down to the beach and played in the water like two little kids. I had a one-piece RCA VHS camcorder that my mother gave me as a high school graduation gift, and I had purchased a waterproof divers bag. It was a cloudy day and the surf a little rough but not too bad.

We took the camera and were pretending it was a boat skimming across the water and diving underneath. If you watched that video today, you would get incredibly sick. We acted like we were shipwrecked, and I was crawling ashore toward the camera and the waves crashing into me and the camera. After a while, we headed back to the swimming pool at the motel. I hung the camcorder on my shoulder. I had forgotten to turn the darn camcorder off and for the next few minutes is footage of me walking from the beach to the pool with the annoying sound of the plastic housing of the bag rubbing against the mic. Only after I got into the pool did I realize it was still recording and turned it off. That evening we played around in the pool with the camcorder and had a great time.

I took my first plane ride with Mike that trip. We went to the Jekyll airport the next morning, paid our money and climbed aboard a single engine Cessna. Mike sat up front with the pilot and I was in the back with the camcorder. Jekyll Island looks a lot different from twelve hundred feet up, so serene and peaceful. We flew over the Clam Creek pier and around the tip of the island to Driftwood Beach. The pilot then took us down the coast flying over the many beachfront homes and our motel. Our flight took us over the golf courses, shopping center, convention center and continued south over Glory Beach, then around the southern tip of the island to St. Andrews beach. We flew over the new Jekyll Harbor marina, the old Jekyll river bridge and the millionaire's village. We then flew out to the Sidney Lanier bridge, the city of Brunswick, parts of St. Simons and finally back to the Jekyll airport. I took this flight a few more times after that. I just love the feeling of being a bird and seeing our beautiful Jekyll from a perspective that only a few people have witnessed.

The next day we went deep sea fishing. We woke up early that morning, had breakfast and arrived at the dock. We climbed aboard, listened to the safety equipment briefing and then we started out. We went out I believe about ten to fifteen miles. This was the first time I could not see land; it was kind of thrilling. The waves were two to three feet with a mild chop. I remember the water being so clear that you could see the fish below us. All of us dropped our lines and the fish started biting. Mike got a bite and jerked his rod so hard that the 10lb lead weight on his line came clear out of the water, flew up in the air and down on top of his head. Blood immediately started pouring down Mike's neck and face. I dropped my rod on the deck, grabbed a towel, applied pressure on the top of his head and had him sit down. After some time, the bleeding stopped, and I could see that Mike had a one-and-a-half-inch laceration right on the top of his head. The captain wanted to call the Coast Guard to pick him up. I convinced him not to because the bleeding had stopped, and Mike wasn't showing any signs of a head injury. After the excitement died down, Mike went back to fishing.

After we got back to shore, I checked on him throughout the rest of the day and that night. Before this trip, I had just completed my eight months training as an Emergency Medical Technician. When we got back to the motel the phone was blinking telling me that I had a message. I called the front desk and it was from my mother. When I called her back, she said that I had received this big brown envelope from the state office of EMS. Nervously, I asked her to open it and she did. She read the letter and said it was my official certification as a Georgia Emergency Medical Technician. I was so happy, and that made my friend Mike my first official patient. Mike and I had a great time at Jekyll. I was glad that he was alright and that I could share the wonders of Jekyll Island and the surrounding area with one of my dearest friends.

My mother and I drove down to Jekyll many times during my teen and early adult years. One of those times was towards the end of August 1995. I remember that miserable drive because we went down as Tropical Storm Jerry was making his way across the state. The storm was supposed to be passed by the time we started out but, it had slowed. We were fine until we left Macon; then the rain hit, hit hard and didn't stop until we got to Jekyll. It was raining so hard in some areas that we had to pull over on the side of the road until it slacked. When we arrived in Brunswick, the rain finally stopped, but the wind was still blowing something fierce and it was cloudy and overcast. We were in 30 to 40mph sustained winds all day until late that evening. We had to take the 20-mile bypass around Brunswick because the Lanier bridge was closed due to high winds and we had to use caution going across the Jekyll river bridge because you would get blown sideways if you weren't careful enough. We also had to be extremely careful opening and closing the car door; The door to our room at the motel would fly out of your hand if you weren't careful and you would get knocked down if you didn't brace yourself against the wind. I couldn't imagine being in a full fledged hurricane. Driving around Jekyll was hazardous too, we encountered many fallen trees and limbs. We even had the occasional power outage. Later that evening, the winds had subsided and early the next day the island cleanup had begun.

My mother has been ill and not been to Jekyll since the fall of 2003. The last time that she and I went together, we took our dog Buster Baxter with us. Buster is a springer spaniel/lab mix with black fur, a white under belly, white paws, and white muzzle with black spots. As he got older Buster started to get separation anxiety. We were staying at the Comfort Inn which was formally the Wanderer. We got up that morning ready to start our day. It was a cool crisp morning. We were going to leave Buster in the room with the curtains open, so he could see out while we went to eat at the Denny's. We had gotten no more than two doors down and he starts barking whining and jumping at the window. Mom turns around and looks at me and says, "were not going to be able to leave him he's causing too much noise". I immediately started regretting bringing him down with us. I went to go and get him, and I put him in the truck with the windows down while we went to go eat. That crazy dog was fine and content with that. He was so scared that we were going to leave him in the room and never return, but he knew we would come back to the truck. When Buster wasn't getting sand burs in his paws or walking on the beach with me, he stayed in the room with mom and I. One day Buster and I were walking around on the beach just past the fishing pier when he saw a blue crab a few feet away down by the water. He runs up to it and started nosing around it and pawing at it wanting to play however, this crab is in no mood to play. It starts backing up with its claws out ready to fight, I tried to hold Buster back so he didn't hurt the crab. He gets a little too close and before you know it, that crab had grabbed ahold of Buster's muzzle and wouldn't let go. Buster started yelping and crying and I grabbed the crab and pulled it off and threw it in the water. After that, Buster wasn't so curious about the Jekyll wildlife.

I brought my wife Kathy to Jekyll Island for the first time in January of 2013. We had just started dating a few months before. One of our first stops was at the Clam Creek pier. We pulled up and it was a cool but not cold day. We went inside the new Jekyll Island fishing center and were looking at all they had to offer. I bought a Choco taco which was an ice cream taco. When I took it outside to eat it, a seagull swoops down and almost steals it from me. Kathy got a great laugh out of that. During that trip, Kathy of course fell instantly in love with Jekyll Island and couldn't wait to go back.

Kathy has a congenital heart defect and has had five open heart surgeries in her lifetime but, that hasn't slowed her down at all. She started having fainting spells and decided it was best to get herself a service dog that she named Gemma. Gemma is a brown Weimaraner/Lab mix and was named after Gemma Teller Morrow on the show *Sons of Anarchy*. She served my wife faithfully for almost two years and then was retired after Kathy stopped having the fainting spells. Gemma, unlike Buster loved the water. After Buster passed away in March of 2017, we took Gemma with us to Jekyll for a short three day stay in May of 2017. We stopped at the entrance towers to get the customary picture that thousands like us have taken and of course Gemma sees the water in the pond and wants to jump in. I hook up her leash and let her wade around and I'm cautiously watching for any alligators that might be around. She enjoys her few minutes in the pond and then I put her back in the truck were riding down the causeway with the windows down and Gemma has her head out enjoying the breeze. We passed the toll booth and proceed to the Quality Inn to check in. Once were checked in; we take Gemma to the beach. There is no one else around so I let her off her leash. I am thinking she's going to be cautious or scared because she's never seen this much water before. But in true Gemma fashion, she jumps in like she's been there a hundred times. Gemma immediately starts swimming out to sea and I'm going in after her trying to pull her back towards the beach. I am up to my neck in the water trying to get her back and she wants to go out further. She's biting at the water as the waves crash into her and she's rolling all over in the sand and generally having a great time. It's not long before she starts throwing up and pooping water. While I go and clean up her mess off the beach, she jumps right back in the water. Kathy calls the vet and they say to give her Imodium. We get her back to the room, wash the salt and sand off her, give her some medicine and she falls asleep in her kennel. We go eat, come back, she's still asleep, wore out from her time on the beach. She wakes up, enjoys her dinner and goes right back to sleep. We take her out to the beach again the next day but watch her closely and take her out of the water earlier than she had wanted. In the few days we were down, Gemma went with us everywhere we went. We kept the engine on with the air running and Gemma dutifully sat in the truck waiting on us. The next day we had lunch at McCormick's Grill at the golf clubhouse. We parked under a palm tree on the edge of the packed parking lot and left Gemma asleep in the back seat. We walk up to the clubhouse where outside the door golf carts are parked all around. We go inside and sit down, and the waitress takes our orders. While we waited, I went to look around in the Pro shop. They had everything an aspiring or expert golfer could ever want collared shirts, pants, shoes, clubs, balls, towels, tees and how-to videos. It was a beautiful day outside mostly sunny, not a cloud in the sky and hot. They have these big bay windows in the back of the restaurant overlooking the putting green and golfers were out sharpening their putting skills. Off in the distance you could see golfers out on the course and in an unused section the sprinklers were shooting great streams of water unto the course.

Inside, players just finishing their round of golf and others about to start theirs are sitting around having lunch. A few other players were having a few drinks while watching the latest golf tournament or the latest news on the golf channel on the various wall mounted televisions. The ladies at the bar are making mixed drinks and pouring beers from the taps or bringing out food orders to the tables. After our meal, we head outside in the blistering sun, back to the truck and Gemma who's enthusiastically wagging her tail and enjoying the cool air inside the truck. The next day, we head back home, and Gemma was back to normal a few days after that.

In the summer of 2016, I was leaving the museum shop one day after a tour of the millionaire's homes and Kathy who had not been feeling too well had earlier taken the truck back to the hotel, to lie down for a while. I told her that after the tour was over I was going to walk back to the hotel and I would see her later. Behind the museum building is one of the holes on the golf course. I decided to walk the course for some exercise. I've never been a golfer however; I knew enough about golf etiquette not to make any noise and if someone was playing in the area to wait until their swing before moving. There were only a few players at that time, so my walk was going at a good pace. It was beautiful on the course. It was a part of Jekyll I've never seen before. Walking along the cart path it was completely silent except for the wind blowing through the pine trees and blowing around loose leaves and pine straw. The birds were chirping, and I heard the occasional small plane fly over. As I was walking along the path, I got about thirty feet from a rather large pond when the water started to stir. An alligator came out of the pond and stopped on the edge to sun itself. It had its mouth wide open. He was staring at me with that toothy grin and I stopped cold in my tracks. I was just about frozen with fear. It was about three to five feet in length but still big enough to make me have a bad day. I started to look around for an exit strategy and then up ahead about one hundred yards, there was a bathroom. I just stared at this gator and started walking slowly away. I've seen plenty of alligators before but, they were either behind a fence or I was above them on a catwalk. I have never been face to face with one with nothing between us but air and opportunity. Luckily, he didn't pay me any mind and I arrived at the bathroom feeling relieved.

I was never a bike rider as a kid I mean I had bikes and all, but I preferred to walk. I did take a bike to Jekyll once. I started out from the Jekyll Estates and headed up to Driftwood Beach. Once I arrived, it was quiet and peaceful. The waves were gently crashing into the rocks and pieces of driftwood. It was an overcast and humid day. As I looked out over the water, I noticed what looked like fog and it was coming towards me; I realized it was a rain shower, It looked like a curtain of water flowing across the ocean and before I knew it, I was in a torrential downpour that lasted about five minutes. I sought shelter under the trees further in from the beach but, I was drenched. After the rain I said what the heck and just continued around the island.

Just passed the Horton House, I was biking along and minding my business when suddenly a doe and her fawn ran across the path in front of me darting into the woods. I locked my bike down to avoid hitting them and I crashed landing on my right-side giving myself a nasty looking abrasion. I had a good case of road rash on my right leg and arm but, luckily no head injury. I got up and dusted myself off and I rode on until I got to the Jekyll Island fire department. By this time blood has covered the bottom half of my right leg and was running into my shoe. I knocked on the door, asked if they could help me and they said, "Come on in."

I sat down in the office and waited while they got some supplies. The station was quiet that morning except for the dispatch radio crackling with reports from the Brunswick and Glynn county fire departments. The

EMT's got my wounds cleaned, removing asphalt and dirt from the bike trail. Once I was all cleaned up, I thanked them and headed back to the Jekyll Estates. After that, I went back to walking, it seemed to be much safer for me.

A few years before this, I was working at the Morrow fire department and we were transporting a patient to Piedmont hospital in Atlanta. When a fire department or ambulance service transports a patient on a backboard to the hospital, they have to stay on the board until cleared by the ER physician. Once that the patient is cleared of having a head or neck injury and is taken off the board, the hospital personnel place the board in a designated area to be picked up by the fire/ems services later. After a while the boards get piled up and there are boards there from all over the Atlanta area as well as some from other parts of Georgia. After our patient was taken care of, I checked to see if any of our department's boards were there. I picked up one from a few weeks prior and put it in the ambulance. While I was looking for ours, I saw one from the Jekyll Island fire department sitting there. I was amazed to see one from so far away. I left it and head back to the station. Later that day after several phone calls to the Brunswick and Glynn county fire departments trying to find the Jekyll fire department number, I called down there to tell them I found one of their backboards at an Atlanta hospital. I explain to them that I will be down there on vacation in a few weeks and I could bring it with me. They said, "please do, that would be great".

The next day after my shift, I drove back up to Piedmont hospital to pick it up the backboard and took it home, I cleaned it up and stored it on our enclosed front porch. This was one of the many trips where it was just me and my mom going. We arrived at Jekyll early that morning and had breakfast at the Huddle house. After breakfast, we stopped by the Jekyll fire department, knocked on the door, the shift Lieutenant opened the door and I explained who I was. They were very appreciative that I brought it back to them. I was a huge fire department patch collector at that time, and they gave me one of their fire patches for my collection as well as a department t-shirt for my kindness. I wore that shirt proudly for many years.

My mother has always told me that as a child and young adult I had a wild imagination. In 1992 I read the book *The Hunt* by Bill Diehl. It is a story about a Nazi superspy that has settled in the United States awaiting orders prior to America's involvement in World War 2 and the story's climatic ending was set on Jekyll Island. After reading the book, my imagination was kicked into high gear. I was visiting Jekyll shortly after reading the book; and in the middle of the night I drove over to the village, got out and started to imagine myself as the super Nazi spy hunter Francis Scott Keegan. I was hunting Nazi Germanys perfect spy, the man of a thousand faces also known as "21". Here I am, a 23-year-old guy, stalking around the village playing the part in the middle of the night trying to catch an imaginary Nazi spy. I am just glad no one actually saw me, and it makes me laugh as I write about it now.

My family and I never spent any real time in the millionaire's village when I was a child. We would ride through and look at the homes. I remember when you could drive down the main road in front of the clubhouse all the way to the end. The huge limbs of the massive oak trees hung so low that they had reflectors imbedded in the limbs to warn drivers at night. This road is now closed to vehicles and is for foot and bicycle traffic only. As a teenager, I started to take a keen interest in the island's history. I would take the tour of the millionaire's village so many times over the years that I could have given that tour myself. I would walk around from home to home, and the clubhouse and grounds and imagine myself as one of the members of the Jekyll Island Club back in the day.

The home I liked the best was Indian Mound cottage. The home has a beautiful wrap around porch. In the past you could walk around anywhere inside the house and even walk inside the big safe that was in the living room. Walking upstairs, the wood of the staircase would moan, groan and creak under your feet and the smell of all the old wood and vintage furnishings throughout the house was fabulous.

What I remember most about the Millionaires village as a kid was the wharf. There was a seafood shop where the Wharf restaurant is now, and you could buy fresh seafood that came right off the boats. You'd walk inside, and the smell of fresh seafood hung strong in the air. The air conditioning and coolers would be humming away and the floors were always wet from the ice. The display cases were filled with different sizes and kinds of shrimp, fish, flounder, blue crabs and scallops all nestled in thick beds of crushed ice and on the shelves were Styrofoam coolers and different seasonings and spices. In these days the docks were filled with shrimp boats and some pleasure craft. We would walk down the dock and watch the men work and unloading their catch to take to market.

In the later years, I enjoyed going to the Clam Creek pier in the late afternoon or early evenings to watch the fabulous sunsets. As I walked out unto the pier, it seems that other people had the same idea. People from all walks of life competing with those out fishing would line the rails with their cameras at the ready to catch that one special photo. The Lanier bridge was almost always the center of any fantastic photo. As the sun sets lower on the horizon, the sky is ablaze with many shades of red and yellow mixed in with the quickly disappearing blue sky. There would be absolute silence on the pier with the exception of the hushed tones of people whispering to one another. They spoke in an almost reverent like tone as if they were attending church. As the sun quickly sets, the sound of camera shutters clicking fills the air. As day turns into night, the sky is now almost dark and the lights on the Lanier bridge are twinkling in the distance.

Just over the Clam Creek bridge and just before you get to the beach area where the Jekyll river meets St. Simons sound there is a concrete road that goes parallel to the beach. It was late afternoon in the early 1990's I started walking down this road. I had never been down it before and so it was a new adventure for me. On the right was Clam Creek and on the left was the maritime forest that backed up to the beach. It was a beautiful walk, so peaceful and quiet. The wind rustled through the trees and the palmetto bushes on both sides of the road moved with the rhythm of the wind. A family of racoons were crossing ahead of me and I stopped to watch them. It was a momma and three of her babies, and they stopped and looked up at me for a moment. We just looked at each other and then they kept walking until they made it to the safety of the bushes.

I continued to walk the road until it ended at the beach about two or three hundred yards up from the old north picnic area. The tide was in at that time and as the waves gently rolled unto the beach and around my shoes, I stood there for a long time and enjoyed the beautiful sight of the sunset shining off of the thunderstorm clouds way out at sea. The oranges, pinks and purples in the clouds, the lightening passing from cloud to cloud and then into the sea was awe inspiring. As it continued to get darker, I realized I had no flashlight. I started to make my way back using what light was left to keep myself on the road and out of the bushes. Luckily, I made it back to the pier before it got too dark. Later that evening, those storm clouds made it onshore and provided us all with a spectacular light show and torrential rainfall.

The Clam Creek pier become my wife's and my observation spot for the great solar eclipse of 2017. There was a guy out fishing and he was catching a lot of baby sharks and throwing them back in. The water became a gray angry color with a mild chop during the eclipse. The sky was overcast and looked like late afternoon/early evening although it was only 2:20 in the afternoon. There was a family out on the pier viewing the eclipse through their special dark glasses and my wife and I didn't have any. They let us look through their glasses. It was fascinating to see the moon partly cover up the sun and its effects here on earth.

In my later teen and adult years, I loved going to St. Andrews in the evening when no one else is out there. I'd walk out unto the wooden ramp and look out across the water toward the marsh then toward the south at the lights of nearby St. Mary's and Kingsland reflecting into the sky. Turning to the north, the lights of Brunswick and the Lanier bridge can be seen flickering in the distance. It is so quiet and peaceful out there, the soft sounds of the waves rippling onshore and the breeze coming off the water. During the hot and humid summer months, I witnessed the lightening from land-based storms flashing and dancing across the towering clouds off in the distance. I would turn to walk off the ramp to make my way back to the truck and then the mosquitoes start their attack. Flying all around my face like fighter planes dive bombing their targets. I fight my way back to the truck and once inside the safety of the truck, I swiftly kill any mosquitoes that made it inside with me and then I head back to the motel. When I am at the entrance to St. Andrews, I turn my headlights out just to see how dark it really is. It is so dark some nights, I can barely see my hand in front of my face I take South Riverview drive and along the way, see the occasional doe with her fawn grazing and a family of racoons or opossums walking across the road. I pass the darken parking lot of the Summer Waves water park and the lone lighted sign that marks the entrance to the Jekyll Marina and restaurant. At the end of Beach View Drive, I turn right unto Ben Fortson Parkway and make my way back to my motel for the night.

I went to Panama City Beach in 1998 with two friends of mine Blake and Reggie, this trip started out bad. On the way down, just outside of

Columbus Georgia, my vehicle was rear ended. The driver wasn't paying attention but luckily Blake and I were uninjured. Reggie was driving his own car down and wasn't involved in the wreck. I had to have my vehicle towed forty miles back to Columbus to the local Chevrolet dealership where I arranged to have my vehicle fixed and picked up a rental car. After a few hours, we finally made it to Panama City Beach. Another reason Reggie had taken his own car was I let them know, when we were planning the trip, I was leaving early to spend a few days at Jekyll before heading home.

On the day I left for Jekyll the North and Central parts of Florida were experiencing the worst wildfires in their history. The smoke never affected us on the Florida panhandle but, when I reached Jacksonville, the smoke was thick in the air and made it hard to see sometimes. This would be the first and last time I ever went to Jekyll Island without making a hotel reservation. When I arrived, nothing was available anywhere on the island and I had to take a room at the Days Inn in Brunswick. The smoke wasn't too bad in Brunswick but, when I arrived on Jekyll, the smoke was thick and hung low in the air everywhere on the island except on the beaches.

Walking around in the millionaire's village and the Clam Creek pier area, the smoke was so thick that the sun beams shown through the massive oak trees looked like beams of light you'd see in a rock concert. It smelled like a campfire that had gotten way out of control and people were just miserable. Your eyes watered and you coughed constantly. It just didn't feel right. I stayed on Jekyll a few more hours that day and went back to my room in Brunswick to go for a swim in the pool and have dinner. Later on that evening I went to bed hoping that tomorrow would be a better day. The next day, I felt even worse about being there. I felt like I was in an alien place and this didn't feel like my beloved Jekyll Island should. I spent maybe an hour on Jekyll and then turned around and went back to my room at the Days Inn and started to pack my bags. Early that Saturday afternoon I checked out and left for home. To help pass the time as I drove, I listened to the Atlanta Braves game on the radio when I could find a station. I arrived home late that afternoon to the surprise of my mother and before I went to bed that night, I prayed and hoped to never again see Jekyll Island like that again.

Like I said earlier, I was never a bicycle rider, but, I love to go walking. One day in the early 1990's I decided to walk the Jekyll causeway. My mother had dropped me off on the marsh side of the Jekyll river bridge and

I began my walk. It was a bright sunny and hot day. The sky was a deep dark blue with white puffy clouds and there was a moderate breeze. I started walking down the causeway and I saw this strange looking object out in the marsh. As you're coming towards the island, it was on the right side. It looked like a flat platform with some kind of antenna on it. The entrance was off the road a few hundred feet before you got to the bridge. I walked down the small roadway and it led to a double gate which was locked. I looked through the gate and down the road that was covered by thick trees on both sides. It was dark down the path and looked kind of spooky even in the daytime. I learned later; the object was a radio navigation beacon for aircraft called a Vortac tower.

Leaving the pathway, I continued down the causeway making sure I stayed on the edge of the road and not too far in the grass because of the small cactus that, in some places covered the area. These cacti were covered with hard very sharp thorns and can easily go right through your shoe and into your foot. In the tall grass these cacti looked a lot like the long ears on the marsh rabbits that called the causeway home. The marsh around the causeway was peaceful and quiet. When there was a lull in the traffic, you could hear the birds singing and chirping in the small bushes that lined the causeway. The breeze felt refreshing as it blew in from the ocean, the river, and across the marsh. The lush green grass looked like waves of grain in a wheat field. I passed the power poles with the X bracing still looking at them with childhood amazement.

I got to the bridge just before the entrance towers. The tide was out because the exposed sea creatures and mud started giving off that rotten egg smell. I stood on the bridge and looked out towards the shipping channel and the Lanier bridge off in the distance. The sky was starting to get dark because a thunderstorm was approaching from the east and by the time I made it to the entrance towers; the sun was now well hidden by the approaching storm and the heat and humidity had diminished considerably. Before my walk, Mom and I had agreed on a time to pick me up, but luckily she saw the storm approaching and decided to come and get me early. I got in the truck and welcomed the air conditioning with opened arms. Going down the causeway back to Jekyll, I looked in the rear window and saw it had started raining at the entrance. The rain was like a curtain traveling up the road toward us and sure enough the storm caught up to us when we were stopped by the Jekyll river bridge waiting on a pleasure boat to pass. It was raining so hard you could hardly see out the windshield and the thunder was rattling the windows. Almost as fast the storm as the storm had hit, 10 minutes later it was gone, and the sunshine heat and humidity returned with a vengeance.

As a child, we never went to the part of the beach that it is now called Glory Beach. I visited Glory Beach one early November morning after I arrived by myself after traveling all night. The sun was just rising above the horizon and it was a clear and cool day. The wind was blowing off the water at a pretty good speed. I was standing at the top of the crossover and you could see the loose sand flowing across the wide deserted beach like waves of grain in a field. The tall sand dunes were standing guard against the wind and waves. You could see from some exposed dunes how the sea oats were anchored in the sand to hold it all together. At the high tide mark, the white sand was mixed with black sand and the ripples kind of reminded me of chocolate and vanilla swirl ice cream. At night you could ride through the area of the soccer fields just off the beach, shine the headlights of your vehicle across those fields, seeing countless deer feeding on the lush green turf and the sprinklers at work watering the fields.

Another place I like going is on the riverside of the island behind the Dubignon cemetery. One of Jekyll's many tidal creeks border the area adjacent to the cemetery. Looking down in the creek at low tide, you can see hundreds of fiddler crabs scurrying all about in the dark mud. The many different types of birds that call Jekyll home arrive at this and the countess creeks to pick up an easy meal. There's a spot right on the edge of the marsh behind the cemetery where you can sit on a bench and look out and see the marsh stretch out for eternity. Looking out across the marsh at night, you can see the twinkling lights of both the city of Brunswick and the Lanier bridge off in the distance.

CHAPTER SIX

Hey kid, turn that damn light out!

Our early years on Jekyll were spent at the Cherokee Campground. Later we stayed primarily at two motels, The Wanderer and Jekyll Estates Inn. Both had great ocean views and were pretty much central to everything on the island. Arriving at night, you first saw the Wanderer as you went around the curve on Beachview Drive right past the last, big, paved, parking area. The end of the building had the Wanderer sign in big letters flanked by a few palm trees that were illuminated by colorful bulbs such as red, blue, green and yellow. Passing by you then saw the big main sign lit up in red neon letters. The motel itself was lit up with yellow bulb lights outside of each door. We would go into the lobby to check in. The lobby had a small gift shop and a television that was always on in the sitting area. After we checked in, we received our key. It was attached to a black plastic oval shaped fob with the motel name and room number on it. Stepping into our room, we would pass the air conditioner humming with the ever-present water puddle just beneath it. The room had that distinct motel smell. I would guess it is caused by the combination of cleaning chemicals and the type of laundry products used mixed in with the muggy tropical atmosphere.

The walls were bare cinder block painted an off white with beams going across the ceiling. In the bathroom, they had the tiny bars of soap wrapped in pink paper and lots of towels. My job was to take the ice bucket and go down to the ice machine and fill it up. Walking down pass the other rooms, the air was thick with humidity. When you got to a breezeway, the ocean breeze came through, would hit you; it felt great. At the ice machine, the scoop was attached to the outside of the machine by a rusty chain and the ice was always that very hard round ice that reminded me of a socket out of a tool set. Right beside the ice machine was of course a Lance snack machine and a Coke machine. I remember going down one time with some friends of ours and they had no rooms available. The front desk clerk took pity on us and gave us the conference room. We slept on the floor in our sleeping bags and had plenty of tables and chairs to sit around. There were beach crossovers right behind the motel at regular intervals and we would go down and spend our days at the beach just like always.

One night in 1979, my father and I were out walking on the beach. It was quite late, and we were heading back. We stopped by the swimming pool which at that time was completely dark and didn't have a fence around it. It was quite crowded for such a late hour. As we were walking around, I turned on the flashlight I was holding and shined it into the pool. Suddenly, this voice yells out, "Hey kid, turn that damn light out"! My father quickly grabbed the light from me, laughing turned it off and said, "Let's get on back to the room son." What my young mind didn't know was, I shined my light on a few couples probably having sex in the darken pool. 1979 was the last time I went to Jekyll with my father before he and my mother divorced the following year. The huge hit that year on the radio was *My Sharona* by the Knack. They played this song it seemed like every thirty minutes and my father loved it. Whenever it came on, he would turn up the radio in the truck to the point of blowing the speakers and drive my poor mother crazy. That Christmas, I bought my father the 45 single and he played it so much until my mother secretly took it, broke it up and threw it in the trash.

We stayed at the Wanderer many times even through several name changes such as Comfort Inn and Ocean Side Inn and Suites. One time I went down with a friend of mine and we were staying on the oceanside downstairs. We had been out and about all day when we arrived back at our room, there was a note on the door that said, "Please do not enter room and come to the front office immediately" We went to the front desk and they said one of the maintenance men witnessed a snake crawling across the porch outside of our room and may have crawled into our room through a small hole at the bottom of our door. We were to go down and being cautious, move our stuff out and they would put us in another room. We go down and start moving our stuff out with no problem, but cold chills were running up and down my spine the entire time. We never found out if they caught the snake or not. If I had of found the snake myself, I would probably have had to change my underwear. They put us in one of the hot tub suites that was on the side next to the Denny's restaurant. You had to be careful in those tubs because they had quite the suction. If you leaned up against one of the water intake ports, it would suck your skin in the port and hurt like crap. Your shoulder would look like you just got a massive hickey on it.

I remember checking out of the Wanderer once long after it had been renamed the Comfort Inn and received a piece of old Jekyll nostalgia with my bill. The cash register the front desk used was the same one used by the Wanderer and the receipts they gave were still stamped with the words Wanderer Motel on them. I thought that was kind of neat.

Between the old Wanderer motel and what is now Tortuga Jacks restaurant, was a stretch of concrete sidewalk called the boardwalk. You had an unobstructed view of the ocean from the boardwalk as you walked down toward the restaurant. They had these concrete benches placed at intervals along the boardwalk that were painted in a teal green or light blue color. I sat on these benches for hours just looking at the ocean or at the stars at night and would be lost in thought. I had sat on one of those benches so long one night that a friend of mine that I had taken down with me almost reported me missing to the Georgia State Patrol. This was well before the days of cell phones and I said I was going out for just a little while and would be right back. I was gone for like four hours and he got worried and was out looking for me. When I finally returned, the look on his face was pure relief.

Later, in my teen years, we stayed at the Jekyll Estates Inn. We did stay once when I was a toddler. I have a picture of me holding on to the railing at the Jekyll Estates and a picture of the pool itself. I liked the Estates the best of all the motels mainly because of the swimming pool and the giant gnarly wind-swept oak trees that provided shade on those hot summer days. The swimming pool here was unfenced and had a wide-open view of the ocean at that time and there was easy access to the beach as well. Swimming around in the pool, you could look up into the trees and see all kinds of birds flying around tending to their nests. On occasion, they would hop on the top step in the pool and take a bath. The ever-present squirrels were always around checking everything out. You could feel the fresh ocean breeze blowing through the trees, hear the humming of the rooms air conditioners and hear the laughter of old and young alike who were splashing about.

The oak trees at night had the same colorful lights as the Wanderer shining up onto the giant limbs. You could stand outside your room at night feel the refreshing ocean breeze and see the brightly lit swimming pool and the trees lit up in red, green, blue and yellow spotlights. Walking along the path past the trees toward the beach itself, it got extremely dark. The breeze was at its strongest here. You could look up into the sky on a clear night, to see millions of twinkling stars and hear the sound of the ocean waves breaking onto the beach. You felt like you were in another world. I stood there and imagined what Jekyll was like long before the millionaires and the state of Georgia came along.

It was at the Jekyll Estates pool where I SCUBA dived for the first time. I traded a handgun to a friend of mine, Greg Bird, that lived in St. Mary's for some SCUBA gear that he had. I took the gear back to the pool and tried it out. My friend Mike Martin was with me. He and I took turns trying it out. We swam around the pool getting use to being underwater and exploring the pool bottom and lights. We would stand on the edge of the pool or sit on the diving board and fall in the water backwards just like we had seen on television shows. We quickly used up the air in the tanks and thus, our SCUBA experience was over.

We never stayed at the Seafarer/Quality Inn across from the street from the Wanderer until years later. We tried it one day just to see how it was and was pleasantly surprised. The staff was very kind and helpful to all needs and this became our hotel of choice for a number of years. We were such regulars; we had the same room four years in a row. Before they renovated, the rooms reminded me of the old Jekyll Estates with the exposed cinder block walls, beams across the ceiling, tightly woven carpet and the old television on the stand. I never minded the vintage look. To me, this was the Jekyll of my youth. In the bathroom they had a regular light and a red infrared heat light in the ceiling. I had a bad sunburn one day and was going to take a shower one evening before going to bed and I made the mistake of turning that heat lamp on. I never made that mistake again, it made my sunburn worse than it already was. This is a pet friendly hotel and made Gemma feel very welcomed the first time we brought her down. The

maintenance man was very helpful with providing me with a garden hose
so I could give Gemma a bath (which she hates) after her ocean swim. They
also had a nice hot and cold breakfast each morning in the meeting room.
They had Belgian waffles made to order, Danish, doughnuts, biscuits and
gravy, hard boiled eggs, sausage, cereal with milk, bagels, toast and fresh
apple and orange juice. They have now completely renovated the hotel and
rebuilt the swimming pool and we look forward to staying with them again
soon.

I drove down by myself in December of 1998. This was the first time I
had ever been to Jekyll when it wasn't hot and humid. It was strange seeing
the motels decorated with Frasier fir Christmas trees in their lobbies and
Christmas lights hung up on the buildings and in the palm trees. This was
well before the huge Thanksgiving weekend festivities they have now. Once
you arrived on the island, they had lighted mechanical deer on either side of
the pay station and some lights in the trees. I also stayed at The Jekyll Island
Club Hotel for the first time on that-trip. It was extremely nice but, it didn't
have the vintage Jekyll feel, I felt like I was staying in a museum. I had been
so used to an oceanfront view for so long I guess I kind of got spoiled. The
food was fantastic though, and I still enjoyed going to the Grand Dining
room for breakfast and lunch.

We never stayed at the Corsair, old Holiday Inn, Carriage Inn/Ramada,
the Buccaneer, Villas by the Sea or the Sand Dollar but, we did go to many
of the restaurants in these motels. Another restaurant I enjoyed eating at
was Black Beards. It sat up on a hill overlooking the sand dunes and the
ocean. The seating area if I remember was long and was divided by a chest
high wall with a replica of a ship's yardarm in the center and various nautical
décor all about. One side had the street view and the other had the ocean
view. The food was excellent as well and it reminded me of the Captain Joe's
seafood restaurant in Brunswick. What really stood out for me at Black
Beards was a waiter named Gart. I never got his last name but, this guy
was fabulous and always deserved a great tip. He was so good in fact that
on a busy night, I would wait until a table opened in his section just to get
him. Gart always recognized me each year I came down. Sadly, just before
Black Beards closed, I stopped by and Gart no longer worked there and had
moved on to do something else.

Sea Jays restaurant at the new Jekyll Marina quickly became our place to eat the first night on the island. We went there because of their famous all you can eat low country boil. Walking inside, you would see the restaurant was small with an intimate feeling. The cash register on a display counter by the door with Sea Jays t-shirts for sale underneath and all kinds of Jekyll memorabilia on the walls, as well as a signed framed movie poster for the movie *Jekyll Island* that was filmed on the island. The steam table was set up against the windows by the door and it was loaded with steaming fresh shrimp, corn, potatoes, and sausage. The next pan held the cole slaw then rolls followed by a pan of banana pudding. As you ate, you had a beautiful view of the sunset with the docks that held pleasure craft of all shapes and sizes; beyond that was the Jekyll river. They had a small bar area with a few stools and in their early days, had a small play area in a corner of the room with toys for children. Sea Jays closed a few years ago and Zachary's restaurant after a few years' absence returned to Jekyll and now occupies the space at the Jekyll marina.

We would eventually go shopping and eat at the Jekyll Shopping center. The shopping center consisted of two separate buildings with bathrooms built later between the two buildings. One building had the same type of roof as the Clam Creek pier, I'd call it a humpback type and the other building had a butterfly type awning colored in teal green and salmon pink. In later years, they covered all of that up with a wooden façade to make both buildings look more uniform in appearance. We would eat at the Jekyll Island Seafood House a few doors down from the Zippy Mart convenience store. You'd walk in and immediately be hit with the wonderful smells of fried fish, flounder, scallops, oysters, crabmeat, hushpuppies, hamburgers and fries coming from the kitchen. In the morning the smells would be of scrambled eggs, sausage, bacon, hash browns, toast and grits. They served the coldest glasses of orange juice I could ever remember drinking. As you walked in, the cash register would be on your left. There would be booths down the walls on each side and tables in the center. The whole place was decorated in dark wood paneling. Against the back wall next to the kitchen entrance was the salad bar. What I remember most about that salad bar was, they had a half of a giant clam shell that held the saltine crackers, captains' wafers and melba toast and in the mornings, they had those small individual boxes of cereal sitting on top of the salad bar.

Later, Zachary's Seafood took over. They still had the same wood panel walls and the giant half of clam shell by the salad bar and the best peanut butter pie I have ever had. Outside the restaurant the racoons would come out from the woods that were right beside the building and on busy nights when the line was out the door, people would feed them. Further down past the restaurant was a laundry mat and next to that was what I call the most iconic store on Jekyll Island *Whittles Gift Shop*. I believe Whittles has been around about as long as the shopping center itself.

Stepping inside Whittles, you were greeted by an extremely nice women Nana Ferguson, she always had a great smile and warmly greeted each customer as they walked in. They had a wide assortment of T-shirts and gifts made from seashells like night lights, little characters, and ships with the sails and trinket boxes made from cedar. They also had cookbooks, writing stationary, postcards and puzzles. As a child, I have fond memories walking up and down the t-shirt aisle trying to find the perfect Jekyll shirt to take home. What I remember most about Whittles was that above their door was a glass panel tinted in blue with the word souvenirs in gold cursive writing. I hope they were able to save that panel before they tore the building down.

The next store I remember was the Jekyll Pharmacy. You'd walk in from the intense summer heat outside and be blasted by the ice-cold air conditioning. You would immediately smell the numerous vinyl toys, floats and beach balls. The windows were tinted a medium blue and on top of display shelves stood vinyl floats, rafts, innertubes and Styrofoam boogie type boards all ready to be used. The shelves were lined with trinkets and Knick knacks made from seashells and driftwood. Further down another shelf held an array of key holders, bill holders, jewelry boxes and funny plaques that were made from cedar wood. Other shelves, held boxes of saltwater taffy, piles of T-shirts, stickers, bumper stickers and racks of postcards. The smell of copper tone suntan lotion mixed in with the smells of a normal pharmacy filled the air too.

After the explosive growth of the internet and birth of eBay, I discovered old postcards of Jekyll and now have amassed a collection of 200+ postcards. Some are the ones I have no doubt I looked at as a child in the pharmacy. After the pharmacy closed, a t-shirt shop moved- in but it didn't have the same charm. Before they tore the building down, there was a shop named Sand Pail Gifts. They carried glass and porcelain figurines and some very nice jewelry. I was standing outside the shop one day and started looking at the window and at just the right angle, you could just make out the old decal residue from the Jekyll Island Cafeteria. I faintly remember as a child going into the cafeteria and helping my mother get a tray and passing down the stainless-steel serving line getting our plates full before sitting down to eat.

I really enjoyed Maxwell's Hardware store. They had an impressive display of Jekyll glass and dishware that graced our dinner table for many years. Walking into Maxwell's today, reminds me a lot of the old Jekyll Pharmacy. They have plastic and vinyl beach toys, racks of t-shirts and other souvenirs that give off that distinctive smell I so remembered as a child. My father's favorite store, of course, was the liquor store out on the causeway. He was very happy about liquor and beer sales being allowed on the island. He and others would get so upset when they left the island to go to the liquor store to buy beer then had to pay another toll to get back on the island.

Behind the shopping center and next to the gas station was in my mother's favorite restaurant on the whole island, Huddle House. We would stop by just after arriving on the island or a few times during the week before we started our day. You'd pull in right off the parkway and into the ample parking lot. The building was nestled in between the massive oak trees that hung low over it and provided shade. In the mornings during the summer, the windows would be covered in dense condensation from the combination of the tropical humidity and the always ice-cold air conditioning inside. Stepping inside and passing the sign on the door that read "No wet bathing suits" you instantly froze from the air conditioning. The old jukebox played whatever a customer had chosen for the hundredth time that day.

The grill would always be busy; covered with orders of hamburgers, sausage, bacon, ham, hash browns and eggs of any kind. The waffle irons would be smoking and churning out waffles and the toasters popping up toast. The coffee pots sat steaming with regular or decaf coffee. The coolers behind the counter had their share of condensation on them too and the dishwasher under the counter would be going constantly. When the washer was opened, the steam would pour out enveloping the poor waitress that opened the door. She would gather the freshly washed hot dishes and stack them above the grill to be used again. Each booth and counter seat would be filled with families, fisherman or island employees enjoying their meals before beginning or ending their day. After our meal, we stepped into the outside air thick with humidity to begin our day. We went down one year only to find the Huddle house had closed and the parking lot taped off with caution tape. Someone said that a branch from one of the massive oak trees fell on the roof during a storm and severely damaged it. We were told the owners had chosen not to reopen. The building sat empty until it and the old Phillips 66 service station were torn down to make way for a new Flash Foods convenience store and Dairy Queen.

I brought my girlfriend at the time; now my beautiful wife Kathy down to Jekyll for the first time in January of 2013. The shopping center was then empty, and all the shops were moved into trailers to a temporary oceanside location while the new beach village was being built. Some of the shop's doors had been left opened or removed and some windows missing. Ceiling tiles and other trash littered the floors. I quietly walked past each space looking in at the bare walls and floors remembering in my own way the many happy memories I had in these stores. As a kid, the stores seemed to be so much larger than they did that day. I imagined them when they were open, full of merchandise and me, as a kid wandering up and down the aisles. My eyes taking in the bright and colorful floats, or t-shirts. When I got to the old Zippy Mart convenience store, that had long since been renamed Flash Foods, the old hard plastic Flash Foods trash can was sitting outside the door. I asked the crew working at the other end of the shopping center who had graciously let me wander around if I could have the old trash can, they said sure take it. It's now on my back porch by our grill. When the new beach village opened, it was good to see some of the old shops like Whittles, Maxwell's and the grocery store come back.

In later years I became a huge fan of the Santa Christmas Shop. I was a firefighter for twenty-two years and over 90 percent of the fire related ornaments I have on my tree come from the Christmas shop on Jekyll. As you walked into the store, no matter what time of year, Christmas music would be playing to put you in a festive mood. They had numerous trees decorated with different themes such as patriotic, sports, rustic, beach, and country. You walked through the store and they had ornaments of all kinds hanging on kind of a board that had pegs like you would hang a coffee cup on and each board had a different theme also. They had a beautiful Christmas village setup. I spent a lot of time one day just looking at each piece of the village that was all lit up. Homes, shops, fire and police station, gas station, theater, schoolhouse, and numerous cars and trucks all almost covered with fake snow. They had old world glass ornaments, small and giant nutcrackers, holiday cd's and ornaments that could be personalized for any occasion. I would take my purchases to the register and the nice lady behind the counter very carefully wrapped each ornament in either white, red or green tissue paper and placed them in a bag. The Christmas shop was originally located in the old Jekyll Island club powerhouse but was later moved to one of the pier road shop locations when the old powerhouse was being renovated to house the Georgia Sea Turtle Center. I was sad to see the Christmas shop had been closed on one of my visits in 2009. It had become one of my regular stops during my trips. Later on, the US postal service took up residence in that location after the oceanside location had been closed. A little further up Stable Road stands the cottage that once housed the Jekyll Island Club infirmary. It was for a long time, home to Jekyll Books. As I said earlier, I am an avid reader and this shop would be one of my first stops when I arrived on Jekyll. Walking up on the wide porch, they had a rack that held discount books for sale and during the summer, fresh ice-cold lemonade sat on a stand by the door. Walking through the massive wooden door you stepped inside, and the smell of vintage wood from the house and books filled your nostrils. In the center of the room, was a table with books on Jekyll Island and from local and regional authors. Along the sides were first editions and signed books. There was a cabinet that held the much older, rare and valuable books. Upstairs, each individual room had its own theme of books and gifts. I never walked out of Jekyll Books without purchasing something and nearly all my collection of Jekyll themed books came from this store. Jekyll books is now closed and the Jekyll Island Museum has taken up temporary residence there until the new Mosaic museum is finished.

One of the pier road shops that's always on my list of places to go while at Jekyll Island is the Commissary. It was here, that I discovered the fantastic taste of Balsamic Sweet Onion Jam. I walked into the shop one day just to escape the heat outside and was immediately hit with the wonderful smells of coffee beans. I am not a coffee drinker but, that coffee smelled great. The smell filled the entire store and they had 12 different flavors you could choose from. I walked around the store looking at all of the BBQ sauces, jams, jellies, salad dressings, and salsas they had available.

I went over to the table where they had samples of jams and jellies laid out with saltine crackers. I saw the Balsamic Sweet Onion Jam; I got a small spoonful and spread it on a cracker. I fell instantly in love with it and bought a jar and took it home with me. When I got home, I instantly regretted not buying more, the jam tasted even better on grilled pork chops, and grilled chicken. I now get a few jars each time I'm at Jekyll.

Across from the Commissary is a new store called "Remember When". I stepped inside and was instantly taken back in time to my youth. The items they had for sale include t-shirts, coffee cups, magnets and plastic motel key fobs with the names of the original motels complete with their vintage logos. They featured the Wanderer, Corsair, Buccaneer, Dolphin Inn, Jekyll Estates Inn and Stuckey's Carriage Inn. Across one wall was a display of reproduced vintage Jekyll postcards for sale. They even had a section of Stuckey's candy with my beloved pecan rolls. They also have a display of original Jekyll Island brochures, matchbooks, postcards, and other items for you to look at. The lady behind the register, Tracy, was very kind and answered any questions we asked. If you want to see vintage Jekyll Island, I highly recommend this store.

The Jekyll Estates Motel as seen from the beach access walkway: 1986
Author's collection

The beach at the Jekyll Island Club beach pavilion: 1998
The sandbar has begun to make one its first appearances
and people venturing out to the edge.
Author's collection

The Author on the Sidney Lanier Bridge: 1995
Note: Construction has not yet started on the new bridge.
Author's collection

Driftwood Beach at high tide: 1993
Note: Concrete and asphalt lining the shore was once the
Roadway into the North picnic area and the Picnic tables
used by countless persons throughout the years.
Author's collection

Mike Martin at the wharf: 1991
This was the day our deep-sea fishing trip.
Note: To the right, the repairing of the dock and construction of
the building that would later become the Latitude 31 restaurant.
Author's collection

Jekyll Island center: 2004
Author's collection

Ocean Side Inn and Suites formally known as the Wanderer Motel: 2004
On this trip, a snake crawled through a small hole at the bottom
of our door, forcing us to be moved to another room.
Author's collection

The Author's Mother and Buster shortly before Buster's
encounter with a crab on the Clam Creek Beach: 2003
Author's collection

On Osprey having lunch at Horton Pond: 2019
Photo Credit: Carol Ann Wages
Reprinted with permission

An Alligator on the prowl at Horton Pond: 2019
Photo Credit: Carol Ann Wages
Reprinted with permission

Author's Wife Kathy and Gemma on the Clam Creek Pier: 2017
Taken shortly after Gemma's first time in the ocean.
Author's collection

The Author's favorite spot on Jekyll to quietly reflect on life: 2017
Note: This is directly the Du Bignon Cemetery
with the Lanier Bridge seen in the distance.
Author's collection

The Author's Wife Kathy with Gemma admiring
the sunrise at The Great Dunes Park: 2017
Author's collection

CHAPTER SEVEN

Day trips to St. Simons, St. Marys and Fernandina Beach

We would spend a few hours one day each trip going over to St. Simons Island to see what was going on over there. Going down the Jekyll causeway, we always played a game that we called count the bunnies. Traveling down the causeway my mother noticed all the marsh rabbits alongside of the road and started counting them, thus starting a game we still play today. The game goes like this, whoever counts the most rabbits, starting when you leave the Jekyll river bridge and reach the entrance towers, wins. You could only play early in the morning because after it got hot, the rabbits would be back in their burrows. Sometimes if the grass hadn't been cut in a while you couldn't tell if you were seeing the long ears of the rabbits or the tops of the small cactus plants that grew along the causeway and resembled the rabbit's ears. After our game, we went over the big bridge and into Brunswick. We passed old, now gone motels like The Oleander, The Palms, and Oak Park Inn. We passed a huge tall smokestack by the pulp mill belching out an incredible amount of steam.

We got on the causeway to St. Simons. Before the new elevated causeway was built, I loved going over the many drawbridges and being stopped by the boats. We then passed the huge marina on the right and onto the island. We traveled what seemed like forever before reaching the Village area where the pier and lighthouse were. Life on St. Simons moved at a faster pace than on Jekyll. As a kid, I didn't really know why until I was able to understand that this was a residential island much like a small town and unlike the state park of Jekyll. The shops in the village had everything we saw on Jekyll, but everything had St. Simons stamped on it.

Out on the pier there were the fisherman, crabbers, sightseers, and others just "people watching". Fisherman out on the pier had their lines cast and were waiting on bites. The crabbers would lower their nets into the water and patiently wait to raise them to see if they caught anything. The fisherman and crabbers had their catches in coolers or in buckets filled with seawater. Tackle boxes were laid open with a wide assortment of colorful lures, reels of fishing line, floats, hooks as big as my little hands, pliers, lead weights and lots of plastic worms present and standing by to be chosen next. From the pier, you would get to see up close the many ships that came in and out of port from all over the world.

On the edge of the village there was and still is a great T-shirt shop called St. Simons Beachwear. They have hundreds of different beach themed decals they can put on dozens of different kinds of shirts. Stepping inside, you immediately smelled the heating irons located behind the counter that transferred decals to T-shirts. They had guys and girls bathing suits, flip flops, beach mats, and of course, suntan lotion. The most popular rock n roll radio station blasted the latest hits over the store's speakers. In later years, I loved going to Frederica Station to look at all the funny signs, t-shirts, floats, shell items, numerous gag gifts. I had so much fun playing with the giant bubble wands outside the store and of course cranking a penny inside of a machine to flatten it out and leave an impression of the famous light house on it. Next door to Frederica Station, was Waterfront Gifts. They had glass and porcelain figurines along with personalized shot glasses, bar coasters, large pencils, key chains, and t-shirts for sale.

I climbed the 129 steps to the top of St. Simons lighthouse once, back in the early 1990's and I took my camcorder with me. At the top there was a great view looking out across the water at Jekyll Island and you could see the northern most part of Driftwood Beach and the Clam Creek pier off in the distance. Just below and to the right of the lighthouse was the casino building with a huge pool that was full of people at the time and that had a black shark figure painted in the center of the bottom. I stood up there with the sun on my face and a nice breeze blowing in from the Atlantic. I imagined what it was like to be a lighthouse keeper in the 1800's having to make that climb several times a day and then looking at this same view. Later, that day when we watched the footage back on Jekyll, there was a beeping noise that I don't remember hearing. I'm guessing it was a radio transmitter of some kind that was mounted above us, and human ears couldn't hear but, the microphone on my camcorder had picked it up.

Leaving the village, we would then head over to Fort Frederica at the north end of the island. On our ride to the fort, we passed under centuries old oak trees draped in Spanish moss. The branches hung so low over the road that they had reflectors attached to the limbs to warn drivers just like the road in front of the Jekyll Island club. Once at Fort Frederica, my parents had to snap many pictures of me sitting on the cannons, posing beside the remains of the old barracks and fort itself all while being eaten by the mosquitoes. They had these information panels all around the fort area. They gave you information on the section of the fort you were in. They reminded me of the desks that we used in elementary school. You walk up to them and flip up the top and a prerecorded message about that section you were in would start playing and would stop once the top was closed. We left Fort Frederica and headed to the battle of Bloody Marsh monument. As a kid all I remembered was looking at the marsh at low tide and being eaten alive by mosquitoes. Other visits to Bloody Marsh in later years were offset with plenty of Off bugspray.

As a kid, traveling down the St. Simons causeway towards Brunswick, I would look out across the marsh and look at the big bridge off in the distance and remember how tall and majestic it was. We didn't do too much in Brunswick in the early days of my youth but, one of the places I remembered we did eat at was Arthur Treachers Fish n Chips and McDonalds out on Highway 17. In later years, we spent a great deal of time in Brunswick. We would go to Walmart to pick up anything that was forgotten during our packing at home or just explore some shops around the mall or the antique shops on Gloucester street or any number of shops around town or on a rainy day go see a movie at Glynn Place mall or The Island Cinemas on St. Simons. After lunch, we headed back across the big bridge to Jekyll.

One day driving up to the big bridge, the steady green light suddenly turned yellow and then red, the yellow caution lights began flashing. The crossing arms started to come down and block our way and a bell started clanging warning us to stop. Off in the distance coming from Jekyll was a big cargo ship. To a kid this ship was enormous. We got out of the truck and everyone else got out of their cars to get a better look. The center span started to rise above the road and seemed like it was reaching into the sky until it reached the top of the four towers. We all just stood by the rails watching as the big ship inch ever so closer to the opening in the bridge. As the ship was going through the center of the span, it seemed like the opening wasn't going to be wide enough for the ship going through it. The superstructure of the ship was taller than the road we were standing on and towered above us all. You could see people walking around on the deck of the ship as it passed. On the other side of the bridge, tugboats stood by ready to escort the big ship to her berth. The ship passed through the opening without incident and as the span started its slow descent down, everyone returned to their vehicles. Once the center span was level with the road, the crossing arms rose out of the way, the bell stopped clanging and the steady red returned to green. We headed back out to Jekyll. We would get stopped by the Lanier and Jekyll bridges many times over the years and I never missed an opportunity to get out of the truck to see the big ships. On occasion, the Lanier bridge would be closed for repairs from either a ship strike or mechanical problems, that meant a twenty-mile detour just to get to Brunswick or St. Simons Island from Jekyll Island. I remember hearing the locals talk of how much time it would take to repair the bridge, that time was often weeks and sometimes months and the reason was I later learned that when a part was needed, it had to be custom made because the parts didn't exist anymore. When the bridge was down for repairs, trips off of Jekyll were limited to one per day because of the distance. When I was down with my friend Mike Martin in 1991, we were coming back from St. Simons and going to Jekyll and we saw a ship coming in from the sea. We turned around and waited by the side of the road until the ship got close enough. We drove out unto the approach and we were first in line when the gates came down. We got out and filmed the ship going through the bridge with the camcorder. This was the first-time Mike had seen a ship so close. He was extremely thrilled. I'm glad I captured it on video for him.

The old Lanier bridge has always captured my imagination, the way it stood there majestically. In later years before it was replaced, I would park just short of the approach and walk up to the lift towers. I had my camera and would get photos and later video of the whole bridge. I loved just standing there looking out toward the entrance to the Atlantic Ocean, feeling the strong breeze hit my face and hearing the sound of the vehicles rolling over the grating. Many times, I wanted to climb up to the bridge tender's booth and ask for a tour, but I never had the nerve. After the new bridge was built, they had started dismantling the old bridge. I was lucky enough to be there and get some photos of the old bridge before it was gone forever.

The southern span was completely dismantled, and part of the old northern approach span is now used as a fishing pier. When the new bridge was being built, I would walk up and just stare at the sheer size of the new bridge under construction. The workers were pouring the concrete for the new massive piers. Giant construction cranes were picking up and setting into place, the rocks for the islands that protected the piers from ship strikes. The construction company had a special machine that was shipped from overseas that would pour concrete and connected the elevated roadway sections. When the new bridge opened to traffic, the old bridge didn't seem as mighty as it once was. It was dwarfed by the newer bridge and sadly there would be no more drrrrrrrrrrrrrrrr as you rolled over the grating. I'm glad I captured the sound on video though. The new bridge in its place is certainly more magnificent looking and safer for both vehicle and water traffic.

One of our other daytrips would be to St. Mary's on the Georgia/ Florida state line. We never took this trip until after some dear friends of mine had moved there. Greg Bird was a very important person in my life. He's the same guy that I traded a handgun to for some SCUBA gear. He was one of my church's first youth student pastors. People that were enrolled in the Columbia Theological Seminary in Decatur Georgia to become ministers of the Christian faith took summer internships at local churches to work with the youth and to help further their educations. After the summer they would be asked to stay on to work with the church's youth year-round until they graduated. It so happens that Greg choose my church Philadelphia Presbyterian Church in Forest Park, Georgia for his summer internship in 1981 when I was thirteen years old. Greg became like a father figure to me after my parents divorced when I was twelve. After he graduated, Greg, his wife Jobeth and their two children Brandon and Charlsie moved to the South Georgia town of Camilla where he took a job as a minister of the local Presbyterian church. I visited them while they lived there on a few occasions.

After a while they left Camilla and then moved to northern Jacksonville Florida where Greg took a job as a minister at a local church. Jobeth was an educator and took a job as a teacher and then head administrator of St. Mary's Middle School. They moved to St. Mary's Georgia while Greg still preached in Florida. My mother and I would go and visit them often and I would take friends that were with me to meet them.

After I graduated high school, I would go down and visit them on my own. They are a very loving family and would make me or anyone else I had brought down with me feel right at home. They introduced us to a great local restaurant called the St. Mary's Seafood House now called St. Mary's Seafood and More. It was here that I first heard of a dish called shrimp and grits. The restaurant reminded me a lot of the old Jekyll Island seafood house. It was cozy and intimate, and they had great food.

Greg also had for a short time a golf cart renting business. You could rent a golf cart and travel around the old town of St. Mary's looking at the clothing, antiques, and book stores. St. Mary's is also the home of the U.S. Navy's Kings Bay submarine base. They also have a submarine museum there in town that has all kinds of submarine artifacts and a working periscope that you can look through and imagine yourself at sea looking for the enemy. Greg and Jobeth still live in St. Mary's and are now both retired and spend a great deal of their time traveling around the country as Greg is a great Blue Grass/Gospel singer. Their children Brandon and Charlsie are now both married and have families of their own for Greg and Jobeth to spoil. Later, we discovered that one of Kathy's cousins David Allwine and his family live in Kingsland, Georgia. We met them one evening at the St. Mary's Seafood House and spent hours talking and laughing and just getting to know my new extended family.

I was visiting Greg's church one Easter Sunday and one of the members of his congregation invited us all to eat Easter dinner at the Timuquana Country Club where he was a member. I remember the day was bright and sunny. The country club was beautiful and very exclusive looking. Members arrived dressed in their Sunday best with their families in tow. We walked inside the Clubhouse, passed the pro shop and into the restaurant. The smell was just fabulous, it made you hungry even if you weren't. It was setup like a buffet and had ham, turkey, dressing, vegetables of all kinds, full salad bar, potato salad, pasta salad, all kinds of bread, any drink you wanted and more desserts than you could ever hope to eat. After we ate, we stepped out into the bright sunshine unto the back lawn which backed up to the St. Johns river and provided us with a beautiful view of downtown Jacksonville. I do not remember the man's name that invited us but, I sure did thank him for inviting me and providing me with such a treat.

My uncle Robert and his family always vacationed at Fort Clinch State Park in Fernandina Beach Florida. We would go down to visit them either on a day trip or to finish out our vacation with them. We packed up our camp site on Jekyll, piled everything in the old, red Ford pickup and headed to Florida. If we left early enough, we would play count the bunnies while driving down the Jekyll causeway. At the entrance towers, we turned left and headed south on highway 17. Along the way we passed homes, trailer parks, mom and pop type restaurants and small motor court type motels, all surrounded by tall pine trees that stood in perfect rows like soldiers at stiff attention. Logging trucks would zoom passed us heading north stirring up loose bark that would pummel the old Ford truck.

In the town of Woodbine, there was a store much like my beloved Stuckey's, called Rawl's. We would always stop; mom would get her beloved pralines and me my pecan roll. They had something else that caught my young eyes. It was one of those wooden birds that you stand on the edge of a water bowl and it magically bowed down and took a sip of water, then rose up again rocking back and forth a few times before taking another drink. Of course, I pestered my poor father until he got me one. I would watch that silly thing for hours.

Further down highway 17, the tall pine trees seemed to close in on the road making the roadway look ever so narrow. Close to the Georgia/Florida state line, we passed an old abandon motel called the Ga/Fla Inn. I knew we were almost in Florida. As we got closer, I saw a light blue draw bridge over the horizon It wasn't a huge draw bridge by any means but, it still made that sound drrrrrrrrrrrr as we rolled over the grating. On the right of the bridge there is a railway bridge that is also a draw bridge.

On the other side, stood a large sign by a roadside picnic area proclaiming "FLORIDA" We always stopped and took the necessary pictures of us at the sign. After interstate 95 was completed, we would take the interstate to exit

373 which was the Fernandina beach exit. Right off the exit was a souvenir/fruit store called the Florida Citrus center. Inside they had everything you could think of funny plaques, bumper stickers, T-shirts, windchimes made from shells, painted coconut heads, fruit and palm trees you could plant at home, all kinds of candy made from coconut and Claxton fruit cake.

In the back of the store they had a giant stuffed six-foot Alligator surrounded by smaller alligator heads for sale. Beside the stuffed gator they had live baby alligators in aquarium tanks swimming and crawling around on the small rocks. Outside under big colorful umbrellas, they had wooden display tables setup with a wide assortment of oranges, grapefruits and other citrus and someone cutting up samples for people to try. Right beside that was a walk up to Dairy Queen. We took highway 17 to Yulee Florida and then east on highway 200 over the Amelia River bridge to Atlantic avenue and then to Fort Clinch State Park.

Inside the park, we stopped at the ranger station to check in. All around us were other vehicles with trailers, -or popup campers attached, and huge motorhomes, all parked and waiting for a camping space to open. The park was always full. We had a few hours before our tent site would open so we went on to the public beach at the end of Atlantic Avenue.

Back in the early days of my family going to Fernandina, they had a small water park by the beach with a couple of slides. You would walk up the stairs and with your flat light blue or teal colored foam mat to sit on. You start flying down the slides and splash into the three-foot pool below. We got quite the workout going up those stairs what seemed like countless times. We would all go down in a train or even backwards or sometimes you'd get knocked off your mat mid-way down the slide.

After what seemed like hours, we finally got to go setup our camp site. Passing the ranger station, the road was very narrow, curvy and long. It reminded me of the road leading to the Clam Creek Pier on Jekyll. Constant shade cloaked the thick maritime forest carpeted with palmetto bushes on one side, while massive sand dunes lined the beach on the other side. As we slowly made our way through the maritime forest we saw signs along the road warning of alligators and other wildlife. We finally reached the riverside campground and it was a lot smaller than Cherokee campground. The camp was in the shape of an upside-down U with camping both inside and outside of the U and the Amelia river was the curve of the U. We had our spot on the inside of the U, and just like at Jekyll, the clanging and banging of tent poles would begin and after a while camp would be setup.

We had a great view of the Amelia river from the campground and would go down to the beach to collect shells. Unlike Jekyll, the beaches at Fernandina were covered in billions of tiny shells no bigger than your thumbnail with plenty of big ones mixed in. I would spend hours looking for the prefect shells to take home while my father was fishing or crabbing. There were signs warning you not to get in the water here. The proximity of the campsite beach to the Atlantic Ocean channel entrance made for some extremely swift and dangerous currents. We had to go over to the oceanside campground to get in the water.

The oceanside campground was in the shape of an oval and was wide open with no shade whatsoever. In the center of the oval were the bathrooms and some picnic tables with grills. People only had their awnings for shade to protect themselves against the intense Florida heat. We would park the truck in a small parking area by the bathrooms and head out to the beach. There was a long wooden crossover bridge built to protect the dunes and many signs warning "Don't pick the sea oats" and "Stay off the dunes." At the end of the walkway there was a short narrow stretch of sand that was extremely hot. Then the wide beach and the Atlantic Ocean was there to greet us once more. In 1975 the popular song *One of these Nights* by the Eagles was a favorite on the transistor radios at Fernandina Beach and the campgrounds at Fort Clinch State Park. We would spend many hours at the beach just like at Jekyll playing in the sand, seashell hunting and witness the occasional sighting of a U.S. Navy war ship. On occasion, you might get a glimpse of a United States submarine traversing through the sound coming from or going to the Kings Bay submarine base in St. Mary's. We would go fishing at the jetties on some trips and we were there in 1978 when they started building the pier that was later destroyed by hurricane Matthew.

We would also spend a lot of time at the public beach at the end of Atlantic Avenue. When I was very young, my father had the bright idea of driving down onto the beach. Of course, he drove too near the water and the truck got stuck in the sand. To make matters worse, it was pitch dark and the tide was coming in. My father gets out of the truck with me, and we started trying to dig out the tires. My mom is in the driver's seat trying to power her way out. All along the tide is coming in and swirling around the tires. With a tremendous amount of luck, the truck gets free and mom drives it further up on the beach and out of danger. I imagine my poor father got an earful from my mother after I went to sleep that night.

I always loved going to Fort Clinch as a child. I would walk through the cavernous halls made from bricks that held the stifling Florida heat like a pizza oven. I stood next to the huge cannons that had wheels that were on tracks, so they could be easily positioned during a battle. I peered through the small gun ports and imagined myself back in another time. I walked through the soldiers sleeping quarters and looked at the bunk beds. When no one was looking, I laid down on a mattress and a pillow that was stuffed with straw, it wasn't very comfortable. I peeked into the hospital that had various medical instruments displayed under glass and medicine bottles in a wooden cabinet. I then made my way back to the top of the fort where my parents were waiting. From the top of the fort you could look across St. Mary's sound entrance and see Cumberland Island. I have read many great books on the history of Cumberland Island but-, I have never been there. I hope to visit there soon.

I remember one evening when Uncle Robert and his family were with us, we were all at the riverside campground. After we had finished eating, we all went to the beach to mess around. I remember seeing what looked like a large pile of sand, I wanted to climb it and see what was on the other side. Uncle Robert told me that King Kong lives on the other side and he might get me. Now Uncle Robert knew I had seen the movie when I was eight and he knew saying that would scare me. I had no intention of going over that hill.

I went back to the riverside campground in the summer of 2017. That so-called large pile of sand was just maybe two or three feet tall. It's like when you have children and they end up going to the same elementary school as you did. You walk down the halls and think, "This place seemed so much bigger when I was a kid." That sandy hill seemed so big as a kid. I had a good laugh.

One day at the Fort Clinch campsite, I think I was maybe five or six, I got up before my parents and got the bright idea that I would make them breakfast before they got up. Now, I've seen my parents light that Coleman stove hundreds of times and thought, "that's easy I can do that." I pumped the piston on the red fuel tank a few times grabbed a match and lit it. I turned the black knob of the fuel tank, nothing happened, I turned the silver handle on the side of the stove and again nothing happened. I turned all kinds of knobs, then I guess I lost interest and just left it. Later when my parents got up, my mom was going to light the stove to make coffee and WHOOF! she was engulfed in a ball of flame that singed her eyebrows and some hair on her head!

My father ran over and pulled her away and the poor stove is just blazing away. He gets the fire put out and sits the scorched stove on a tree stump for a while, letting it cool off. I got my butt tore up. That stove was scorched beyond belief, but it still worked perfectly. It was used for many years after that. Needless to say, I never tried to cook breakfast again on my own.

One other time at Fort Clinch Park, when I was really young, I had developed the mumps and was completely miserable. My parents had decided it was best to head on back home a day early. I was in the cab of the truck crying in pain and my parents were breaking down camp. Suddenly, a big rainstorm came up and they got drenched. I remember sitting in the truck and listening to the rain just beating down on the roof unrelentingly. I watched through the rain streaked windows as my parents franticly ran around outside throwing everything in the back of the truck. I remember that day as a long and miserable ride home.

I was down at Jekyll on the first anniversary of 9/11. I had arrived a few days before and was staying in an oceanside room at the Comfort Inn. On that morning, I was getting ready to take a ride down to Jacksonville Florida and take the Budweiser brewery tour. I was in my room watching replaying of the 9/11 coverage on WTOC TV out of Savannah. At 8:46 A.M. the moment American Airlines flight 11 crashed into the North Tower, I stepped outside my room to snap a few pictures of a lone palm tree on a bright sunny day back dropped against the calm and peaceful Atlantic Ocean. I was working at the Morrow fire department that day in 2001 and we just got back to the station from a fire in an automobile paint booth. The fire was out before we arrived on scene and we made out a fire report for the business owner. Back at the station, I was taking my gear off when one of the lieutenants came running outside and told us that a plane had crashed into one of the World Trade Center towers. We rushed inside and like millions of others watched events unfold on tv for the rest of the day. I still occasionally look at that picture, thinking about September 11, 2001 and what I was doing when I heard the news. I wonder if someone else was staying in that room that morning watching the horror unfold on television and at some point, stepped outside and had this calm peaceful view during that terrible day.

I have first heard about or watched other famous news events while at Jekyll;- In May of 1996, My mom and I were staying at the Comfort Inn and getting ready for dinner when we heard that a ValuJet airliner had crashed into the Everglades shortly after takeoff from Miami Florida, everyone on board was killed. I also watched, on the tv at Brogens bar and restaurant at the Saint Simons village, the famous slow speed chase in Los Angeles involving O.J. Simpson. I also watched a Space Shuttle launch while sitting in the beach pavilion on Jekyll. Although, all you could see was a white trail of smoke in the distance on the horizon. It was still exciting to watch.

CHAPTER EIGHT

Heading home

Mornings when we were to return home, I was sad but kind of glad to be going. My father was the kind of person that didn't mess around; he was a firm believer in once the vacation was over, it was over. It's time to get home as quickly as possible and return life to normal. I still do this today much to the disdain of my wife Kathy. While my mother was packing up the kitchen stuff, my father and I started taking down the tent. The sleeping bags would be rolled up and taken outside with our pillows and that old brown suitcase. All the dark soil and leaves that had accumulated inside over the last few days would be swept from the inside of the tent; the window screens would be zipped up and the front flap closed. Then the song of banging and clanging tent poles would begin. The tent would be folded up and placed under the plywood bed in the truck as was the Coleman stove and cook set. My father put away what was left of the boxes of food, stored the cooler and made sure the lanterns were cooled off enough to pack. We did one last check of our campsite to make sure nothing was left behind and that the campfire was out. We climbed into the truck and went to the camp store to check out. We walked inside the camp store and it was busy with all the hustle and bustle of other people like us checking out, mixed with new campers who were checking in.

Walking out of the camp store after checking out, I would look around the area trying to soak up enough memories to last until our next visit.

After we left the campground, we would then do what I called our farewell tour of the island. We'd drive around to visit everything one last time until our next visit. We walked out on the pier, drove to the North picnic area, visited the Horton's, drove through the Millionaires village, rode past the shopping center, past the motels, and finally St. Andrews picnic area before heading off the island.

I would already start to miss Jekyll. Going home we only made a very few stops. One of those was highway 341 north of Lumber City, Georgia. There was a small picnic area much like the one at the Florida state line. They had the same concrete picnic tables they had on Jekyll. The tables were scattered all around, each with trash cans and grills. Beside the picnic area was a little store called Livingston's. It was a small mom and pop type grocery store that also sold fruits and vegetables. We walked inside and there was an extremely nice elderly lady that stood behind the counter. Behind her was a small room with a single bed and a display sitting on top of a cabinet with dozens of spools of colored thread. We purchased a few tomatoes, some potted meat, crackers, and drinks. We had lunch in the picnic area. Cars of all sorts and logging trucks zoomed by us as we ate. After lunch we continued towards home.

As we passed through each town, I would start to miss Jekyll island a little more. Once we got on interstate 16 westbound headed towards downtown Macon, I would turn in my seat and look across the highway median to see the Golden Isles exit sign one more time. This would be the last reference to Jekyll or the Golden Isles I would see until our next trip. Traveling north on Interstate 75 thru Forsyth and Passed Yogi Bears' RV park, passed the Tradewinds motel, headed towards the Atlanta metropolitan area until we reached our exit number 77 Old Dixie Highway. We turned off and a few miles later pulled into our apartment complex and started unloading the truck. Mom would start the laundry and my father put all the camping gear in storage until it was time to bring it out again. I would unpack my trusty suitcase and store it under my bed.

Later, once we were rested from our trip, and the laundry was done. Mom and I took the film that we shot from the old Kodak 126 camera to the local Eckerd Drug store for processing. While mom filled out the form, I scanned the shelves behind the counter looking at all the yellow, black and red packets of processed Kodak film awaiting to be picked up. Eckerd's Pharmacy smelled almost the same as the Jekyll Pharmacy and I would close my eyes and pretend I was back there. Mom got the claim ticket and I held on to it for dear life. This was well before the days of one-hour photo processing and I knew it was going to take a week to get them back. I looked at the ticket on the way back home just dreaming of when we will get the call, the call to come pick up our next batch of Jekyll Island memories to take home and put in the old photo album. That night as I lay in my bed, having trouble falling asleep, I would relive the past few days we had on Jekyll and pretend I was back in the tent or the hotel room. I would get so far in thought, I thought I was actually there, and I would fall right to sleep. I would get up the next morning and get ready to go to school and I would proudly be wearing the latest Jekyll shirt I had gotten that past weekend.

In later years and still to this day when we stay at the hotels, Kathy and I will pack up the night before except for the clothes we will wear the next day. When I am at Jekyll, I am always up at the crack of dawn. Long before my wife awakes, I either go out on the patio or down to the beach to shoot photos of the always amazing sunrises. I am always out early enough to give the condensation that forms on the lens of my camera time to dissipate. As the sun rises above the horizon, I am firing away with my trusty Nikon camera. I sometimes go out to Driftwood Beach for sunrise photos, but its best if you have someone with you. The gnats and pesky little bugs called no-see-ums will eat you alive that time of the morning unless you have someone constantly fanning you as you're shooting.

After the sun is well in the sky, I will go over to the Horton House and go behind the DuBignon cemetery to look out across the marsh. There is a wooden bench there now and I just sit there and think. This is my alone time and just for me. I will leave it at that. After I get back and Kathy is up, we pack up the truck, have breakfast at the Beach house restaurant and then head on our way towards home. We play count the bunnies as we ride down the causeway, passing the toll booth and the welcome center that is already busy with the day's visitors. Once we're over the Lanier bridge, I look out across the marsh to get one last glimpse of beautiful Jekyll Island. We turned left at fourth avenue then right on Newcastle, pass the state docks and through the old part of town. We continue up highway 341 crossing under interstate 95, then head out of town.

Earlier in this chapter, I wrote about the routine on the mornings we would go home. Just like my father, I would not mess around and get right home. There were only two occasions that I didn't do that. Once in early

2006 I was at Jekyll by myself. On the day I was to return home, was the starting day of the weekend long Peaches to the Beaches Yard Sale. This is an annual yard sale that runs from Perry to Brunswick Georgia. I didn't have to be at work for a few more days and wasn't in any hurry that day, so I made a day of it. I started at the old convention center and in Hartley hall. Each Jekyll resident that was selling had a table or section setup with everything they were selling. After I left Jekyll, I stopped at a few places in Brunswick. I made stops in all the towns on my way home. Some towns would have a few tables here and there while others had entire parking lots or ballfields covered in goods to be sold.

The yard sale was over for me once I left Eastman and highway 341 and then picked highway 23 to Macon. A few miles before arriving in Macon, my next-door neighbor Henry called to tell me that their oldest daughter, Lakyn had fallen ill earlier that week and was in a hospital in Atlanta. Lakyn was 13 at the time and was a sweet, precious and beautiful young lady with blonde hair and green eyes. On the way home, I prayed for her speedy recovery and for her family. I arrived home at six o clock that Friday evening and started unpacking and sadly early that Saturday morning I received news from Henry and Lakyn's mom, Kelly, that she passed away during the night. It was a sad homecoming for me.

The second time I broke the "get straight home" routine was when I took my then girlfriend Kathy down to Jekyll for the first time. She has two brothers, Michael and Bobby, and because they both lived in South Georgia at the time, she didn't get to see them or their families very often. On the day we left Jekyll, Kathy asked if we could go by and visit them. Michael and his wife Laurie lived in Waycross Georgia. We met them for lunch at a local restaurant there and spent some time with them at their home. They had a large, beautiful, secluded home with a nice size fishing pond behind the house. It was a cloudy and cool day and the pond was smooth as glass. We walked around, and Kathy told me stories of when she would come down and go fishing with her brother. We left Waycross and then went to visit her oldest brother, Bobby, and his wife Denise and their children Elizabeth and Cameron in Tifton, Georgia. We arrived just before the end of the school day. We picked up the kids at school with Denise and then went to their home for a visit. We had dinner and then dessert at a gourmet cupcake shop that was a favorite of Elizabeth, Cameron and Kathy. We left a few hours later and arrived home around eight that evening to the barks and happy tail wagging of our two dogs Buster and Gemma. It took a great and special woman to make me deviate from a long-standing family tradition and Kathy is that special woman.

CHAPTER NINE

A long-awaited day trip to Jekyll

Ever since I could drive on my own, I have always wanted to go on a day trip to Jekyll Island. The urge was always the greatest for a week or so after my last visit and then it would slowly go away. One day a few months after the Atlanta Olympics in 1996, I was working part time for a print shop delivering printed materials to various hotels and businesses in the Atlanta area. I had gotten off early that day and the "Jekyll Bug" was biting me. After I got home around 4:30 in the afternoon, I jumped in my truck and headed to Jekyll. Of course, I got as far as Eastman and had second thoughts. I stopped there at the Eastman Huddle House, had dinner and then headed back home. I was back home around 9:30 that evening feeling defeated. I kind of felt like my parents and their first attempts at going to Jekyll so long ago. For twenty-two years I thought about a day trip then, a week before my 50th birthday when we were trying to figure out what we were going to do, my wife Kathy says, "you've always talked about a day trip to Jekyll so, let's do it". I thought about it for all of five second's and said, "let's do it."

6:30 AM on Friday, September 7, 2018, we leave our home in McDonough, Georgia. We follow the same route we always have. However, traveling down interstate 75 the Yogi Bear RV park is no longer there and the Tradewinds motel in Forsyth is gone also. Arriving in Macon, we go on through no longer stopping at the Pierce Avenue exit but now stopping at the Chevron station right off exit number 6 on interstate 16. We arrive in Cochran and go straight through the town. The college is still there as is my former childhood business, and in Eastman the Stuckey's building is still there but now sits empty.

The Carriage Inn across the street has long since been torn down and an empty lot in its place. Helena, McRae, and Hazlehurst are still the small towns they once were but now a little busier. The Hazlehurst radio station WVOH is no longer the local country station it once was. Livingston's store outside of Lumber City is long closed but the building is still there, and the picnic area is long since closed with the concrete tables and grills removed. The town of Baxley still, - holds its local charm and those huge piles of logs are still there. The drive- in where, in the late 70's, I saw *Rocky 2* playing is no longer there, but there is now a great restaurant called Captain Joe's Seafood in its place.

That stretch of highway 341 between Baxley and Surrency is still flat as ever and the caution light in Surrency is still flashing. The towns of Graham, Pine Grove, Odom, Sterling and Gardi are still small, quaint little towns. The town of Jesup still has the building that had the towel and tog shop has long since been abandon. Brunswick has grown into a large town with many major retailers. A lot of the stores in the old town district have changed names but, it still has its small-town appeal. Traveling down Newcastle Street and onto fourth avenue it seems time has stood still. It still looks the same as it did when I was child, except The Building supply building on fourth avenue is now gone. Turning right onto Highway 17, I can still look out across the marsh in eager anticipation of seeing beautiful Jekyll Island. The old B&W warehouse is still there but has a new name. The old Sidney Lanier Bridge was replaced in 2003 with a newer, bigger, and even more majestic looking bridge that is much safer for the larger ship traffic that enters Brunswick Harbor. Turning left on the causeway, there are two beautiful ponds with huge signs proclaiming Jekyll Island. Passed the entrance towers, there are still the power poles with the X bracing between them and the liquor store long since moved on the island has been replaced with a beautiful new welcome center and Georgia state patrol post. We arrived at the automated toll booth at 10:26am, pay our toll and head on. Over the new Jekyll River bridge completed in the mid to late 1990's. Again, arriving on Jekyll, time seems to instantly slow down. Going down the parkway and around the island, I remember how things once were. We pulled up to the Holiday Inn and see about making reservations for next year. We stop by Horton Pond to enjoy the peace and serenity of the area and to snap some photos of the ever-present alligators and turtles. We met an extremely nice woman, Carol Ann Wages, taking pictures at Horton pond that day. Carol lives in Brunswick and travels to Jekyll almost daily to capture some of the most beautiful and dramatic wildlife shots I have seen taken at Horton pond and throughout Jekyll. Luckily, she posts them regularly on the "Friends of Jekyll Island Georgia" Facebook page for all of us to enjoy.

We stopped at the Clam Creek fishing pier to look out over the Jekyll river towards Brunswick and the Lanier bridge. It is a hot and sunny day with a few people out on the pier fishing. We have lunch at the Wee Pub in the new beach village shopping area. After lunch, we then go to St. Andrews picnic area next and I show my wife, Kathy, the famous rope swing. Much to my amusement, she starts swinging on it, singing the Miley Cyrus hit, *Wrecking ball.* We go to the Millionaires village next to find the Island Sweet Shop and get my mother some of her beloved pralines. Just stepping inside this shop will make you gain ten pounds. The sweet scent of chocolate, sugar and caramel just fills the air. Behind the glass display case was every assortment and combination of fudge, chocolate, caramel, peanuts, peanut butter and pecans imaginable. They had hand dipped ice-cream in about eight different flavors and had all kinds of regular candy available too. Stepping out of the sweet shop, we looked for the famous Marty Jekyll, the pier road shops cat, but never found him. He was probably hiding. The whole area was in a buzz getting ready for the Shrimp n Grits festival happening the very next weekend. Workers were out cutting the grass, trimming trees and setting up portable toilets for the festival. We then go to Driftwood Beach once the site of the Old North Picnic area. This is where my sister Jessie and I scattered our father's ashes at dawn after he passed away in September 2010.

On that trip, my sister Jessie and I left my house at 2:00am just like our father would have. This was the first time my sister and I had been together alone in a long time. She is mother to three wonderful daughters Kristina, Destiny and Cierra and a wonderful son Christopher. She doesn't have too much free time on her hands. So, on the ride down, we talked about ourselves as kids, how her kids were doing and what was going on in our lives today. Before we knew it, we were in Brunswick. We had breakfast at the Cracker Barrel and then headed out to Jekyll. Once we arrived on Jekyll, we went out to Driftwood Beach. The sun was just starting to rise above the horizon, the day was promising to be a beautiful day and it was slightly breezy. We went up to the water's edge, opened the cardboard container and dumped my fathers' ashes onto the rocks in the water. The wind blew back blowing ashes all in my face and mouth. "Thanks a lot, old man" I said. My sister was hysterically laughing at me as I am spitting out ashes and dusting myself off. We stood there together watching the sun rise and remembering our father in our own way.

Then we spent the rest of the day hanging out at our motel or out shopping for souvenirs for the kids before returning home the next day. The old north picnic area was very special to me and those are among my most cherished memories of Jekyll Island. I have tried many times to explain to my wife Kathy how the old picnic area looked but its hard to imagine the roadway cut through with those concrete picnic tables, trash cans, bathrooms and grills all about with squirrels, racoons, the ever-present seagulls, and other birds looking for handouts.

On my wife's and my daytrip, we spent just about two hours at Driftwood Beach sitting on an old tree stump looking at the incoming tide crashing into the rocks and driftwood; and watching other people enjoying the area. I sat there thinking to myself, how many of these old trees that are now driftwood had provided me with shade when I was a child so many years ago? Looking out across the sound towards St. Simons, the view hasn't changed much either. The lighthouse still stands its eternal guard protecting ships that enter or leave the port of Brunswick. It was getting late in the afternoon and we had to leave. We stopped at the Flash Foods to fill up the truck. As we are heading down the causeway, we could see the *Emerald Princess* casino boat starting its nightly run with hopeful gamblers aboard dreaming of a big payday. Kathy and I have dinner at the Marsh Side Grill restaurant just below the Lanier bridge. After dinner, we uncharacteristically take the interstate all the way home and arrived in McDonough at 11:00pm that evening tired but happy. I had finally done it; I went to Jekyll Island and came home on the same day. The next day I found out why my wife didn't want to stay overnight at Jekyll, she had planned a surprise birthday party for me at Padre's, my favorite Mexican restaurant. A lot of my family and close friends were there. It was a great birthday.

Kathy and I were able to share the wonders of Jekyll Island with a dear childhood friend of hers Heather. Heather, along with her teenage son, Landon, and her boyfriend, Justin had taken a weekend trip to Tybee Island in August 2018. Heather told Kathy later that day on the phone, it wasn't what they expected. The beaches were extremely crowded, and it was impossible to find a place to park without getting your vehicle towed away. Kathy told her about Jekyll Island and that it was about an hour south of them. "Go check it out" she said, "you might like it". Heather told us when they got back home, "We arrived on Jekyll on a Saturday afternoon and it was like you arrived in another world. The beaches were not crowded, and parking was so much easier. We parked at a spot called The Great Dunes park and went to the beach. There were maybe thirty to forty other people on that part of the beach but, we felt like we were the only ones out there."

"The beach was wide, and free of overwhelming crowds. It was just as beautiful as you described, and we stayed there almost until dark." Kathy and I asked, "How did you like the rest of Jekyll?" Heather said, "We didn't go anywhere else." "We stayed at the Great Dunes park the whole time we were there." We began to tell them of the other things to do on Jekyll and they have already begun making plans for an extended visit in July 2019. We told them about Lewis Baker's Facebook page "Friends of Jekyll Island Georgia" and they have already joined. They love the many pictures that have been posted and can't wait to post some of their own. We also told them of the Jekyll Island legend "Once your feet touch the sands of Jekyll Island, you will always come back" Heather told us, that once her son Landon graduates from high school, she and Justin might retire on Jekyll. Kathy and I are so happy that Heather, Justin and Landon already love Jekyll as much as we do, and they haven't even seen all of it. We told them; they are in for a real treat. I guess that legend is correct after all. Jekyll Island is indeed a very special place to be shared with the people you love and care about.

CHAPTER TEN

A Few Final Words

After all the visits I have ever made to Jekyll Island, I have always wished at one point or another that I could live on the island or at least in the Brunswick area. Years before the old shopping center was torn down, I would go to the laundry mat to pick up and read the latest edition of the island's newspaper *Jekyll's Golden Islander*. I would lean against the folding table and read as my clothes are being washed and dried. On hot and muggy days, when the heat from the dryers would get unbearable, I would go and sit in a booth at Zachary's restaurant and eat a piece of peanut butter pie. I flipped through the pages and read the latest island news and looking on the back two pages at the homes and condos for sale and dreamed one day I would live there. However, in later years, I felt this would be a mistake on my part. To me, half of the fun of traveling to Jekyll Island is getting there.

Before I go to Jekyll, I plan our trip months in advance; where will we stay, what will we do each day, where will we eat etc.? I have been doing this for years it's just habit and half the plans involve just getting to Jekyll. I couldn't even go to Jekyll with anyone else other than myself or my own family. In my teen years when my church youth group would go to the five-day Christian get together called *Fun in the Son* I would never go with them because when I would go to Jekyll, I went on my own terms and no one else's. I wouldn't be able to do the things I wanted to do, when I wanted to do them. I know that sounds selfish in a way, but I had been to Jekyll so many times prior to that, I just couldn't go without going my way. Even when president G.W. Bush hosted the G-8 Summit on nearby Sea Island in

2004, I was asked by my Fire Chief David Wall, if I wanted to go down and work Fire/EMS for the event. I said, "no". I just couldn't do it. I believe that access to Jekyll Island was restricted during that time due to the extensive security concerns for the backup personnel for the leaders of the nations in attendance. That helped me make my decision. Although, I believe I could never live on Jekyll but, I believe I could live close. Due to my wife's heart condition, we can never be too far away from her doctors at Emory University Hospital in Decatur, Georgia so, in the near future we plan on moving to just above Macon, Georgia. That way we can still be close to Kathy's doctors and be a little closer to Jekyll. If it were up to me, we would probably live in Eastman.

When I am not there, I think about Jekyll Island so much that I see and smell things almost every day that remind me of this beautiful little island. I came across a reminder one day and depending on how you look at it, it was either an indirect or direct link to Jekyll Island. When I saw this link, I couldn't think about anything else but Jekyll. When I worked at the fire department, on my days off, I would substitute teach for a local school system. One such day, I was in the bathroom in one of the newer schools and discovered the sinks and toilets came from the Crane Plumbing company. As I am washing my hands, I'm looking at the logo on the sink and instantly think about Jekyll Island Club member Richard Teller Crane and his beautiful home Crane cottage. I remembered that his business was bathroom fixtures. I now see things I normally wouldn't pay too much attention too. It's amazing how many businesses and schools in the Atlanta area have Crane fixtures in their bathrooms.

My wife and I were in a store one day that had a display of Yankee Candles. We walked over and started smelling the many different scents, I picked one up called *Sun and Sand*, took a whiff and it instantly brought me back to Jekyll Island. The candle smelled just like the Copper Tone suntan lotion I spoke so highly of in this book. I keep one regularly on my desk to burn while working. While writing this book, I had one burning many nights for inspiration.

We as humans are creatures of habit. If I were to go to Jekyll any other way than the way I've always gone, something would feel out of place and it wouldn't be the same. Although taking the interstates 75 to Macon and 16 to Savannah and then 95 to Brunswick is a much faster route, I still get off at exit 6 on interstate 16 and pickup Ga highway 341 in Eastman and I love it. I love seeing how much the little towns have changed over the years and how they have grown. I know what's around ever single corner and turn, and I still get excited when I see it. I love the anticipation of coming into Brunswick and seeing what has changed and what's stayed the same. I still travel past the state docks on Newcastle street and turn left unto Fourth avenue. Although it's a blistering hot humid day most of the time when I go, I roll the windows down in my truck to smell the salt air mixed in with the sulfur smell. I have the Bryan Adams hit *Heaven* playing on my stereo as I travel through Brunswick and out on the Jekyll causeway. All of that would be ruined for me if, I moved there. It's the magic of Jekyll Island and the surrounding area that keeps me coming back. It's the people that are so nice and not in so much of a hurry. Being on Jekyll Island, takes me back to when I was a kid with not a worry in the world and for a few days each year I get to relive that. As a child I use to be amazed that people actually worked and lived on Jekyll; and that kids like me lived on Jekyll and had to go to school. I would see the school buses on the island, kids getting off and I would think; those poor kids have to go to school in this paradise. As I finish up here, I've already made our reservations for the Holiday Inn for this summer. The day before we leave, I will have started packing my samsonite duffle bag with my clothes and three rolls of quarters for the laundry. I can't forget the Nikon camera or the cooler full of bottled water, a few beers, a gallon of sweet tea and my wife's bag. Come on Kathy hurry up if we leave now, the GPS says we'll arrive by 3:00pm, "I bet I can beat that". We'll arrive just in time to check in, go for a walk on the beach and get in a dip in the pool before dinner. We jump in the truck. Before we leave we say a prayer for a safe, fun trip and then we are on our way once more to fabulous Jekyll Island..........................

THE END

ACKNOWLEDGEMENTS

This book would have not been possible had it not been for Mr. Lewis Baker and his Facebook page "Friends of Jekyll Island Georgia". Fans of the Jekyll Island page numbering more than 24,000 at this writing post their vacation photos, videos and swap valuable information pertaining to Jekyll Island for the enjoyment of all of the page's friends. It was on this page that someone began writing stories about their youth and teen years during the 1950's and 60's while working and living on Jekyll. As I read these stories, it had awoken some old memories of Jekyll that were in my mind. One night in early 2018, I posted one of three stories about my time as a kid on Jekyll in the early to mid-1970's. My first story was about the sights and smells of the old Jekyll Pharmacy. As I started writing, the words just flowed from my fingers and on to the keys of my smartphone. The response I received was astonishing,

I received many kind words and messages about how the detail of my story brought them back to the pharmacy in their youth. I wrote two more short stories about nights watching the shark fisherman on the Clam Creek fishing pier and camping at Cherokee Campground. A number of people wrote back, you tell a great story with a lot of detail and you should write a book about your memories, I bet a lot of people would enjoy it. After that, I thought about writing a book off and on for the next eight months even speaking to my wife Kathy about it. Kathy was excited about the idea and said go for it, then finally one night a week or so after Halloween 2018, I decided to attempt to write. Now, I've always been an avid reader and can lose myself in a book fast and I can easily spend many hours in a bookstore just looking around. I've never seriously thought of myself as a writer. I started that night and just like that first story earlier in the year, the words flowed from my fingers onto the keyboard then onto the screen of my computer. Writing surprisingly came to me very easily. I would go into our spare room that we call the computer room and shut the door and start writing. On that first night, I didn't come out until four hours later. Other nights it would be two to three hours or until our two dogs, Gemma and McKenzie would whine and scratch enough at the door that I would let them in, or my wife came in to tell me to go to bed because I had to get up early for work the next morning. I would just start writing and couldn't stop. I would lose all track of time when I was writing about my memories of Jekyll Island.

Thank you to my beautiful wife Kathy for being very understanding and the many hours I missed being with you hiding away as I wrote and edited this book and for always being by my side no matter what. Thank you to my Mom for all of your help and to the many family and friends that allowed me to use your names in my book. Thank you to my cousin Spanky and his wife Terri for helping me with certain details and storylines. Thank you to Lisa Stonica for showing my manuscript to your son Brady. Thank you Brady for being brutally honest in your critique going through my manuscript and editing it. Thank you also to my Mother in law Becky Earls for doing a second edit and clearing up those pesky loose ends and making sure everything read perfectly. What you have just read was written completely from memory. There were minimum written notes and no outlines. As I was writing, this book just came together on its own. I hope that you had as much enjoyment reading this as I have had writing it.

ABOUT THE AUTHOR

Jeff Foster retired as a Fire Fighter for the city of Morrow Georgia after 22 ½ years of fighting fires, working EMS and teaching fire safety to countless toddlers, school children and adults. He is currently a 911 first responder in Atlanta Georgia.

He is an avid reader of books on famous historical events. His favorites are first person accounts of World War 2 and natural and man-made disasters.

Along with his wife Kathy, Jeff attends Community Bible Church where for the last six years they have been active members of the on-line ministries team. Most Sundays you can find them "in the booth" surrounded by camera, sound and recording equipment.

They live in McDonough, Georgia where they enjoy spending time with their nieces, nephews, fur babies, Gemma and McKenzie and of course visiting their beloved Jekyll Island.

Printed in the United States
By Bookmasters